The Philippines
In Search of Justice

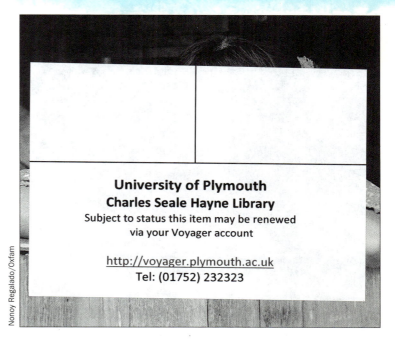

Nonoy Regalado/Oxfam

Charlie Pye-Smith

Contents

front cover: Nonoy Regalado/Oxfam

Oxfam UK and Ireland

Published by Oxfam UK and Ireland

© Oxfam UK and Ireland 1997

A catalogue record for this publication is available from the British Library.

ISBN 0 85598 334 5

Formal permission is required for all such uses, but normally will be granted immediately. For copying in any other circumstances, or for re-use in other publications, or for translation or adaptation, prior written permission must be obtained from the publisher, and a fee may be payable.

Published by Oxfam (UK and Ireland), 274 Banbury Road, Oxford OX2 7DZ, UK (registered as a charity, no. 202918)

Available in Ireland from Oxfam in Ireland, 19 Clanwilliam Terrace, Dublin 2 (tel. 01 661 8544).

OX418/RB/97
Printed by Oxfam Print Unit
Oxfam (UK and Ireland) is a member of Oxfam International.

Nonoy Regalado/Oxfam

Tricia Spanner/Oxfam

Nancy Durrell Mckenna/Oxfam

clockwise, from top left:

- Danao Bay. Palm-fringed beaches and coral sand make the Philippines a tourist paradise.

- Terraces make it possible to cultivate steep hillsides

- Coconuts are grown commercially in certain areas, but everywhere, they provide an instant drink.

- Planting rice, Central Luzon.

- Jeepneys are a rapid and convenient form of public transport in the Philippines.

- Manila. Beneath the advertising hoardings and modern buildings, poor people have built their homes on a narrow strip of riverside land.

Nonoy Regalado/Oxfam

Nonoy Regalado/Oxfam

Nonoy Regalado/Oxfam

Introduction

With its spaghetti of highways, its vast shopping-malls, and billboards promoting everything from Marlboro cigarettes to evangelical Christianity, much of downtown Manila looks little different from Los Angeles. In the cities of the Philippines, the American influence is paramount, and for the middle classes all the amenities and amusements of Western consumerism are readily available. But poor Filipinos inhabit a very different world.

Hernari Monares and his large extended family live in a shack made out of wood, canvas and scraps of polythene on Payatas rubbish dump. One of the older members of the family is too ill to work; several are too young. The rest spend their days picking over the surrounding mountain of refuse in search of plastic, which they sell to a junk-yard nearby. The rubbish-pickers have lived so long in this foetid environment that they no longer seem to notice the stench, or the flies which swarm across their skin.

'We sleep here, we eat here, and we get a living here,' says Hernari, whose 'hog's heaven' t-shirt is an apt description of the site. 'That's why we stay.' As a teenager Hernari worked as a farm labourer on one of the islands in the central Philippines. 'In those days,' he recalls, 'we earned eight pesos a day working in the fields. We couldn't live on that, so we came to Manila.' Until recently the family lived and worked on Smoky Mountain, Manila's infamous rubbish dump, but since its 15,000 squatters had been evicted — as part of the city's recent beautification programme — they had moved to Payatas dump in neighbouring Quezon City.

Tricia Spanner/Oxfam

Nonoy Regaldo/Oxfam

The rubbish-pickers face many problems: Hernari's five children cannot go to school, as the nearest school is too far from the dump; they must walk 400 yards to get drinking water, which costs one peso a pail; there are periodic outbreaks of cholera, dysentery is ever

above, top
Street scene, Manila.

above Hernari Monares in front of his home.

3

present, and the only health clinic in the area is open for just half a day a week. However, Hernari says that his family is much better-off here than they would be had they stayed in the countryside. On a good day they can make 100 pesos, sometimes double that, which is more than the statutory minimum wage for day-labourers in the Philippines.

Over a third of the eight million people who live in Metro Manila are crammed into slum housing, or live precariously in makeshift dwellings on rubbish dumps, railway sidings, and land earmarked for industrial development. Some of the urban poor have been here for generations; others, like the Monares family, are recent arrivals. Nearly all came to Manila in the belief that they could make a better living. This flight to the city is a perennial feature of life in the Philippines and it is a reflection not so much of the wealth that is to be found in the cities, as of the poverty and inequities which prevail in the countryside.

Poverty in the Philippines has little to do with lack of natural resources — the country is rich in minerals; has, or had, plentiful supplies of timber, fertile farmland, and lakes and coastal waters

teeming with fish — but much to do with the way in which these resources are shared. Two-thirds of the rural population are landless. Tribal communities have been driven off their ancestral — and untitled — lands into remote regions where they struggle to make a living. Peasant fishing communities see fish stocks decline as mechanised trawlers take an ever-greater share of the catch.

This short book looks at the problems which stem from the unequal distribution of resources in the Philippines, and at the many-faceted struggle to put right historic wrongs. It looks at the plight of the Manobo and B'laan tribals of Mindanao and at the fishers of Batangas, at the rubbish-pickers of Metro Manila and at farmers who have lost their land to volcanic eruptions and floods; but the story it tells is by no means unremittingly gloomy. It is impossible, as an outsider, not to be astounded by the resilience and cheerfulness of the Filipino people, as they struggle to improve their lot. They are used to hardship, whether it results from bad government or capricious nature. The future is often uncertain, but people are seldom without hope.

right children play in a stream, Sison village, Pangasinin province.

Nonoy Regalado/Oxfam

People from some of the many different ethnic groups living in the Philippines.

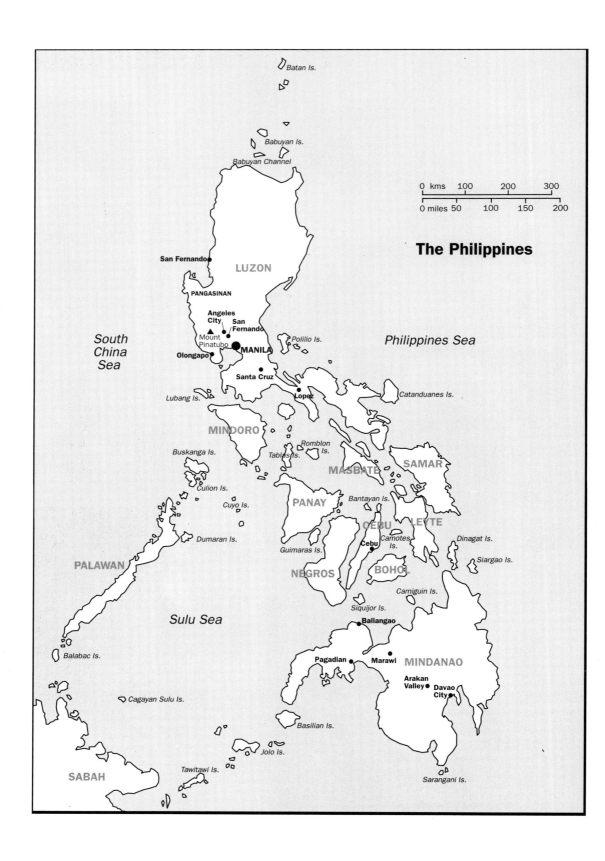

Batan Is.

Babuyan Is.

Babuyan Channel

The Philippines

San Fernando

LUZON

PANGASINAN

Angeles City
San Fernando

Mount Pinatubo

MANILA

Olongapo

South China Sea

Santa Cruz

Polillo Is.

Philippines Sea

Lopez

Catanduanes Is.

Lubang Is.

MINDORO

Romblon Is.

Buskanga Is.

Tablas Is.

MASBATE

SAMAR

Culion Is.

Cuyo Is.

PANAY

Bantayan Is.

CEBU

LEYTE

Dumaran Is.

Guimaras Is.

Cebu

Camotes Is.

Dinagat Is.

Siargao Is.

PALAWAN

NEGROS

BOHOL

Camiguin Is.

Siquijor Is.

Sulu Sea

Ballangao

Balabac Is.

Pagadian

Marawi

MINDANAO

Cagayan Sulu Is.

Arakan Valley

Davao City

Basilian Is.

Jolo Is.

SABAH

Tawitawi Is.

Sarangani Is.

6

The feudal past

The Filipinos, it is sometimes said, are Malays who have spent 350 years in a convent and 50 in Hollywood. The Spanish turned the Philippines into the only Christian country in Asia, while the Americans bequeathed to their one and only colony a taste for consumerism and fast food. The Spanish influence is to be found in the names of places and people, in the architecture of some of the older settlements and, most significantly perhaps, in the way in which the countryside has been carved up by the political elite. A government survey in 1988 found that of the 3,919,000 families involved in agriculture, 60 per cent were landless, 26 per cent owned under three hectares each, and less than 0.1 per cent owned over a quarter of all land-holdings of 100 hectares or more. It is this skewed pattern of land ownership, stamped on the country by the Spanish, which has shaped the political history of the Philippines.

State and church were in league from the very beginning of Spain's Pacific endeavour. In 1565, 43 years after he had first set eyes on the island of Samar in the company of Ferdinand Magellan, the Augustinian friar, Andres de Urdaneta, returned as navigator to an expedition led by Miguel Lopez de Legazpi. The *conquistadors* swiftly asserted themselves and the Philippines became a Spanish colony. During the early years of colonial rule, the Spanish government evinced little interest in the country's agriculture; rather, it saw the Philippines, with its archipelago of 7,000 islands, as a stepping stone on the way to enter the spice trade, which was dominated by the Portuguese, and as a base from which to launch a proselytisation campaign in China. Indeed, when it was suggested to Philip II that the Philippines should be abandoned on economic grounds, he retorted that he would rather spend all the gold in the Spanish treasury than see the loss of one oratory where Christ was praised.

The Philippines' pre-Hispanic past is hazy, and has no written history, but enough is known to build up a picture of the half a million or so people whom the Spanish subjugated. There are clear arguments to suggest that Negrito tribes like the Aeta were the first settlers. Over the millenia migrants from such diverse places as the Indonesian archipelago, Indochina, and China added new blood to the Philippine stock. When the Spanish arrived the majority of people were The

below Taal, Batangas. The Spanish tradition is apparent in some older buildings.

Nonoy Regaldo/Oxfam

hunter-gatherers and slash-and-burn farmers, and most lived in villages or *barangays*, which were founded on bonds of kinship and ruled by *datus*, as they are in the remote tribal areas today.

Two centuries before the Spanish arrived, merchants from the Middle East introduced Islam, which began to supplant pagan beliefs in some communities, especially in parts of the southern island of Mindanao. As far as the Spanish friars were concerned, all non-Christians were infidels and they immediately set about the task of converting them. At times they used force, but many Filipinos willingly espoused the Christian faith, some of whose core beliefs were similar to those they had previously held. The pagans, like the Christians, had a supreme deity and believed in life after death.

More revolutionary than their faith, in many ways, were the friars' concepts about the ownership and use of land. Hitherto, the islanders had had no notion that land could be owned by individuals. The friars were quick to establish freehold property rights and appropriate much of the most fertile land for themselves. By 1898, when the Spanish were ousted, the religious orders owned vast haciendas.

The royal grants of land to *conquistadors* and friars in the early years of Spanish rule were intended to be only for unoccupied land. However, the majority of grants were used to take over settled areas as well, and as time passed many of the big estates swallowed up land which belonged to individual *barangays*. The idea of land as a commodity remains

Nonoy Regalado/Oxfam

Religion is an important part of life for the majority of Filipinos.

above Roman Catholic Church interior;

right fishing boat, Batangas.

Nonoy Regalado/Oxfam

left Statue of the Virgin Mary presiding over a relocation site for people displaced by the eruption of Mount Pinatubo.

anathema to most of the indigenous peoples, but it provided the opportunity for a local elite to emerge. Most were either well-educated Chinese and Spanish *mestizos*, or *cacique*, descendants of the *principalia* who had been involved in tax collection and government service. Many made their fortunes in plantation agriculture and by the 1850s were significant exporters of cash crops like sugar, tobacco, abaca, and coffee.

The struggle for freedom

The latter half of the nineteenth century saw the emergence of a small class of educated middle-class Filipinos: the *ilustrados*. The term Filipino originally meant Spaniards born in the Philippines; now it referred to all those who lived in the archipelago. Best known of the *ilustrados* was Jose Rizal, who was one of the founders of the Propaganda Movement which agitated for reforms and independence. Rizal was executed, but his dream of nationhood inspired the uprising in 1896 against Spanish rule.

By a quirk of fate the revolutionary war against Spanish colonial power in the Philippines coincided with the Spanish-American war which began over Cuba in 1898. The United States Asiatic squadron received an order, while in Hong Kong, to attack the Spanish navy in the Philippines. This it did, and the Spanish fleet was destroyed in the Battle of Manila Bay. The US force blockaded Manila and awaited the arrival of land troops from California. In the meantime the Spanish governor promised reforms in return for support from the Filipino revolutionaries, but the leaders of the movement, having received assurances from the Americans that they had come as liberators, not conquerors, urged their followers to support them against the Spanish. A volunteer army defeated Spanish forces and besieged Manila. On 12 June 1898 Emilio Aguinaldo declared Philippine independence.

The Americans failed to keep their word. In December 1898 the Treaty of Paris, under which the Spanish-American war was concluded, ceded the islands to the United States. The Filipinos reacted by declaring Aguinaldo president of the First Philippine Republic, and the country was plunged into another war. By 1902, when the war ended, over a quarter of a million Filipinos had been killed in one of the bloodiest of colonial encounters.

The Americans, once established, were relatively benign colonists, at least in comparison to the Spanish. They set up a school system which offered education to most of the population — today 90 per cent of Filipinos are literate — and a system of government which ensured that Filipinos were involved in the running of the country. They also separated the powers of church and state.

The revolution of 1896 reduced the authority of the friars, but did little to challenge the system of land tenure. The *ilustrados* who led the revolution were bent on expelling the Spaniards, not on introducing democratic reforms. As an occupying force, the United States, rather than weakening the position of the landed oligarchy, seemed to strengthen it. The only reform of significance, introduced to appease peasant unrest, was aimed at the land held by the friars, who, by 1902, had agreed to sell 90 per cent of their holdings. Instead of giving the land to the 60,000 share tenants farming these estates, the US government decided to sell it: most went to existing landowners, and at least one large block went to a US sugar corporation.

In 1935 the Philippines was granted Commonwealth status, a ten-year transitional period of self-government in preparation for full independence. The United States continued to control foreign policy, but the nation's internal affairs were regulated by elected members in an upper and lower house. There were sporadic rural reforms, again in reaction to widespread revolts among the landless peasantry, but little land was redistributed. By the time the Japanese invaded the Philippines in 1942 the landlords were as powerful as ever. Three years of Japanese occupation caused immense hardship for the people of the archipelago: Americans and Filipinos died in large numbers, both in the lengthy and ultimately unsuccessful attempt to resist the Japanese in 1942, and in the guerilla encounters which continued till the eventual liberation of the Philippines towards the end of 1944.

The Marcos years

The post-war history of the Philippines has been dominated, until recently, by revolt and repression. When Ferdinand Marcos was elected president in 1965, he promised to introduce wide-reaching social reforms, including the redistribution of land. He claimed that by 1969 over a third of a million share tenants would be given leasehold to the land they worked; in the end less than a tenth of that number received written contracts. During Marcos's second term of office the government faced widespread opposition. Maoist-inclined intellectuals and a disenchanted peasantry gave tacit, and sometimes direct, support to the New Peoples' Army (NPA), the military wing of the banned Communist Party. The Communists waged a guerilla war throughout the Philippines, and government forces were also fully occupied in Mindanao, where a Muslim group, the Moro National Liberation Front (MNLF), was fighting for independence. Student unrest and riots in the capital gave Marcos the excuse he needed to declare Martial Law in 1972.

The Philippines slipped into a dark age: political parties were banned, freedom of speech and assembly were suspended, opponents of the regime, whether among the intelligentsia or the rural guerilla movements, were imprisoned, tortured, and sometimes murdered. Many disappeared; thousands remain unaccounted for. Some optimists hoped that Martial Law would provide Marcos with the perfect opportunity, and the authoritarian means, to redistribute land, but more land was taken from large landowners during the year and a half before the declaration of Martial Law than during the following nine years. The only landowners to lose significant amounts of land under the reforms were those whom Marcos saw as political opponents.

Since the mid-1970s, the Philippine economy had been locked into a cycle of boom and bust, with periods of growth being swiftly followed by decline and

Nancy Durrell Mckenna/Oxfam

above Head of President Marcos moulded in concrete on a hillside in the north of the country.

facing page, top
Young worker in the sugar-cane fields, Negros. Sugar cane is grown widely as an export crop, but the market collapsed in the 1980s because of competition from subsidised sugar beet from North America and Europe, causing great hardship among workers in the areas dependent on sugar-cane plantations.

facing page, bottom
The American influence is all-pervading, particularly in the towns.

11

depression. The extravagant borrowing of the Marcos regime, coupled with low export growth, was largely to blame for this inherently unstable state of affairs. Another major factor was the heavy dependence of local industries on imported equipment, which led to constant trade deficits, financed by borrowing. During the 1970s the foreign debt rose from $2,297 million to $17,252 million. The Marcos loans did little to improve the lot of the poor. Frequently they were channelled into grandiose development schemes such as the building of the Westinghouse nuclear reactor in Bataan, which has never been used. A significant portion of the money borrowed was siphoned into the bank accounts of Marcos and his cronies.

EDSA and beyond

The middle classes and poor alike became increasingly disenchanted with Marcos's 'constitutional authoritarianism' and his failure to alleviate poverty, while his allies abroad, most notably the US, gradually lost patience with the dictator. In February 1986 the beleaguered president ordered a snap election. The opposition united behind Corazon Aquino, widow of former opposition leader Ninoy, who had been assassinated at Manila airport in 1983. After a violent and corrupt campaign, Marcos's Commission on Elections declared him the winner, a

below The nuclear reactor at Bataan.

verdict confirmed by the National Assembly, which he controlled. The opposition also claimed victory and less than three weeks after the elections tens of thousands of Aquino supporters blockaded two military camps along Manila's Epifanio de los Santos Avenue (known as EDSA for short). Two of Marcos's most trusted military leaders, General Fidel Ramos and the defence minister Juan Ponce Enrile, sided with Aquino, as did key elements in the armed forces. On 25 February Aquino was declared president and the Marcos family was flown into exile in Hawaii, leaving behind a country burdened with debt and 3,000 pairs of Imelda's shoes.

Cory Aquino saw out her term of office and survived six attempted coups. Her government went some way to improving the civil rights record of the country, but insurgency continued in the countryside, the economy stagnated, the poor remained poor, and the landless, for the most part, remained landless. Aquino restored democracy, albeit with a strong military flavour, but she failed to satisfy the clamour for social change. 'After Aquino took over,' recalls a Catholic priest who works among the indigenous peoples of Mindanao, 'there were such high expectations of reform. We believed that the indigenous people would at last be given control over their ancestral lands; that agrarian reforms would give land to the tillers. But it never happened, so the struggle continued.'

In 1992 Fidel Ramos won the presidency, following a surprisingly peaceful election. Confronted by the very problems — debt, poverty, insurgency, and corruption — which his predecessor had failed to tackle effectively, he declared that his main aim was to turn the Philippines into a 'tiger economy', capable of competing with powerful neighbours such as Taiwan and Malaysia.

John Clark/Oxfam

Philippines 2000

Liberalisation, deregulation, and the introduction of incentives for foreign investment have been the principal tools of reform, which has been carried out under the slogan *Philippines 2000.*

The slogan has certainly been a success — it is emblazoned across school roofs, road signs, car number plates, and city gateways — and economic indicators suggest that in certain respects the country is catching up with its ASEAN (Association of South-East Asian Nations) neighbours. GNP rose by 7 per cent in the first half of 1996, and inflation declined to single figures. In 1995 there was a 30 per cent increase in export growth, and debt-servicing fell from around 40 per cent of export receipts in the late 1980s to 13 per cent by 1996. The Philippines is no longer on the list of countries with a major external debt problem, although the overall debt stock continues to rise in absolute terms, and the spiralling consumption of mainly imported luxury goods by the middle classes, coupled with widespread tax evasion, results in a high current account deficit. However, the International Monetary Fund (IMF), whose three-year programme of reform ends in 1997, has expressed itself more than happy with the Ramos government's achievements in attracting foreign investors and bringing about relative economic stability.

Ramos can also point to some success in the field of social reform, and he has achieved what many believed impossible: a peace settlement with the Moro National Liberation Front (MNLF), the largest of Mindanao's Muslim separatist groups. Since 1972 over 100,000 people have died in the fighting; with the advent of peace comes the prospect of development.

But what of the poor? How have they benefited from *Philippines 2000*? They remain, for the most part, marginalised and dispossessed. Thirty-five per cent of the country's rapidly expanding population — 68 million in 1994 — live in absolute poverty. Fifteen million have no access to health care; 20 million are without sanitation and 11 million have no access to clean water. During Ramos's rule, the Philippines has fallen 16 places, from 84th in the world in 1991 to 100th in 1995, on the Human Development Index drawn up by the United Nations Development Programme (UNDP). A third of Filipino children below the age of five are underweight, which is a higher proportion than is found in Mali, Burkina Faso, and Zaire — three of the poorest countries in the world.

below People living in the port area of Manila are worried that they might be evicted from their houses to make way for industrial development.

Nonoy Regalado/Oxfam

The proportion of babies born underweight in the Philippines is the same as in Niger, which comes bottom of UNDP's Index. Unlike other 'Asian tigers' such as Singapore and Malaysia, the Philippines has failed to translate rapid economic growth into government spending on education and health. Consequently the benefits of economic success have failed to reach the majority of people.

For many of the poor, *Philippines 2000* remains little more than government rhetoric. For others, the policies it promotes are heaping further hardships on lives already made precarious by poverty, by the ravages of nature — 24 million Filipinos, mostly the poor, were affected by cyclones between 1991 and 1995 — and by the inequities of land distribution. *Philippines 2000* may be creating a tiger of the country, but for many life is still ruled by the laws of the economic jungle, where the rich and powerful prosper, and the poor languish in obscurity.

below Antenatal clinic. Many women do not receive adequate antenatal care, and maternal mortality is high as a result.

below, right Mothers and their children at a health class in a slum area of Manila.

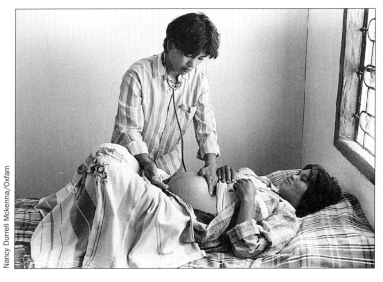

Nancy Durrell Mckenna/Oxfam

Nancy Durrell Mckenna/Oxfam

The last frontier

Talk to any of the older fishing people along the coast to the south of Manila and they will tell you the same story. 'Twenty years ago,' says one in Lian, a small village on the edge of sugar-cane country, 'we could get 20 or 30 kilos of fish every time we went out to sea. Now we're lucky to get three or four kilos.' Further south the people of Salong have seen their catch decline just as dramatically. In the words of one of the leaders of its women's group, 'There have been weeks go by recently when we haven't even caught a scale.' A similar tale is told by many of the freshwater fishers in the Philippines. In the early 1970s the men of Cuenca used to catch up to 7,000 *tawiles*, one of Lake Taal's delicacies, on each trip. Now they often return with none at all.

Philippine fishing villages are the stuff of tourist brochures: colourful *bancas*, the traditional outrigger canoes, push out to sea from long sandy beaches; bamboo huts with pretty flower gardens are clustered about sandy alleys lined with coconut palms, bananas, and other fruit trees. But the picturesque scenery conceals a multiplicity of problems.

There are an estimated one million working fishers in the Philippines with some 4-5 million dependents. Of these 100,000 are paid labourers working on commercial fishing-vessels. Another 200,000 or so are employed in aquaculture, mostly prawn farming; and the remainder — 700,000 — are artisanal fishers who ply their trade in small boats.

Traditionally the coastal zone has been seen as the last frontier: marine resources were perceived as belonging to no-one, and therefore exploitable by all. When

Nonoy Regalado / Oxfam

above Outrigger canoes, or *bancas*, in Batangas. More than a million people make a living from fishing, but stocks have declined sharply in recent years.

communities inland faced destitution or hunger — through typhoons, crop failures, whatever — they would often decamp to the coast to try their luck. Coastal communities were often part-time fishers: it was the land first, the sea second. The older men of Lian and Salong recall that a single fishing trip used to yield enough fish to feed a family for several days: they could afford to be farmers who fished, rather than full-time fishers, as most are now.

The reasons for declining catches fall into three main categories. First, the large-scale commercial sector, including foreign fleets, has taken ever-greater quantities of fish. Second, industrial pollution, siltation, and clearance of coastal mangrove forests have impoverished the marine ecosystem. Third, the artisanal fishers themselves have adopted destructive methods of fishing.

The failure of protective legislation

In 1975 the nation's disparate fishing laws were brought together and updated in a single Fisheries Code, or Presidential Decree (PD) 704. The code divided the sea into two zones: the 7-kilometre municipal zone was reserved for artisanal fishers, the waters beyond for commercial vessels over three tonnes. PD 704 was designed to bring about an increase in production for export. Consequently, it favoured commercial fisheries and aquaculture. Under the new code Marcos also gave foreign fleets from Japan and Taiwan equal rights with Filipinos to fish the country's commercial waters. These rights were reciprocal, but Taiwanese fleets were in a far better position to exploit the Philippines' fish stocks than the relatively under-capitalised Filipino fleets were to exploit Taiwan's already overfished waters.

Trawlers frequently flout the law and fish within municipal limits and coastguards have neither the capacity to

apprehend them, nor, it seems, the will to impose the law effectively when they do. Coastguards often accept cash or a crate of fish from trawlers which are fishing illegally and turn a blind eye to their activities.

In 1918 over 450,000 hectares of mangrove forest fringed the coast. Less than 140,000 hectares survive today. Mangroves have long been felled for fuel-wood but PD 704 hastened their destruction; vast tracts were cleared during the 1970s and 1980s to make way for prawn farms. The loss of mangroves, which are important spawning grounds for many species, has had a serious impact on fish stocks. A hectare of mature mangrove can yield 100 kilos of fish, 75 kilos of shrimps, and 25 kilos of crab, as well as good quantities of shellfish and sea cucumber, every year. When converted to fish-ponds, the same hectare would provide only a month's paid work to a fish-farm worker. The profits from prawn-farming go to private investors, and foreign exchange is earned from exports.

Such was the centralised nature of the legislation that those municipalities which opposed the clearances were unable to introduce their own protective ordinances. However, the Department of Environment and Natural Resources (DENR) has recently introduced legislation which prohibits the cutting of mangroves. This is not uniformly enforced, but the pace of mangrove destruction has decreased.

In the mid-1980s, artisanal fishers still accounted for three-quarters of the total catch. By 1992 their share had fallen to 39 per cent in terms of volume and 33 per cent in terms of value; by comparison, aquaculture accounted for 39 per cent of the total fisheries income and the commercial sector for 28 per cent. The artisanal fishers themselves are partly responsible for the decline in fish stocks, and many of them recognise this.

Nonoy Regalado / Oxfam

A survey of 100 fishers in Danao Bay, in northern Mindanao, posed the question: 'If you experienced a decline in catch, what would be the reason for this decrease?' Thirty-two cited the fact that there were too many fishers; 18 blamed dynamite fishing and the use of poison; 16 thought the use of small-mesh nets was to blame; only 14 blamed commercial fishing vessels. Small-mesh nets caught juvenile fish; dynamite and poison destroyed coral reefs, which, like mangroves, are important spawning grounds; and, most poignant of all, too many people were now going after the same fish.

However, the situation is far from hopeless. Over the past decade, experience has shown that local communities, given the will and the means, can manage their marine resources in a sustainable fashion.

A model for the future?

Fifty years ago there were over 800 hectares of mangrove in the 2,279-hectare Danao Bay. Today a quarter of the original mangrove forest survives, and much of this has been degraded. During World War II Japanese soldiers used explosives

to kill fish. The practice caught on and much of the bay's coral reef has been destroyed as a result.

In 1991 the Pipuli Foundation — Pipuli means 'put it back' — decided to set up a marine protection programme in Danao Bay. From the outset it saw this as a community venture and enlisted the support and help of the mayor, village priests and the fishers themselves. In July 1991 a municipal resolution led to the establishment of a 70-hectare marine sanctuary with a 25-hectare buffer zone. Nine of the 11 fishers who operated fish corrals within the sanctuary agreed to move, were hired as guards, and helped to delineate the boundaries by sinking bamboo stakes into the sea bed. The two fishers who opposed the scheme were given substantial compensation to move out.

Within the sanctuary are two small core areas, one is pristine mangrove forest, the other a depression rich in coral. These serve as fish hatcheries and are off-limits to all, including the project staff. Fishing is not permitted within the sanctuary. In 1993 diving surveys found 48 species of fish and 28 species of invertebrate

above The lines of bamboo stakes mark out the sanctuary area of Danao Bay, within which fishing is not allowed. Fish stocks have built up rapidly since the sanctuary was set up.

macrofauna, including sea cucumber and shellfish of commercial value. Two years later the biologists found 85 species of fish and 75 species of macrofauna in the same area. The density of fish had also doubled outside the sanctuary.

Arjan Heinen, a Dutch marine biologist, has been working in the bay since 1994. 'Figures like these don't convince the people at all,' he says with a wry smile. 'What does is the testimony of other fishers who now see a rise in their catch.' In 1995 the sanctuary was enlarged to 239 hectares and it is now recognised by the government as a protected area, Baliangao Wetland Park.

Saving the mangroves

'Back in 1965, when I was a young girl,' explains Laida Agan, 'there were a lot more shellfish and sea cucumbers in the mangroves of Danao Bay than now.' She attributes the decline to over-exploitation. 'Too many people are collecting now,' she says frankly, 'and some of the methods used are destructive.' Instead of probing the mud with a knife, some collectors plough through it with large implements, destroying the juvenile shellfish and other sea life.

Laida was one of the first to get involved with Pipuli and she did much to convince her fellow collectors that they needed to safeguard the mangroves. Sixty shell-collectors and fish-trap owners have now formed a co-operative, KATUMANAN, and with Pipuli's help they have drawn up a Mangrove Stewardship Agreement (MSA). Destructive methods of collection will be banned and the forest will be zoned for different activities. Since 1995 members of KATUMANAN have been planting mangroves. 'If we don't,' says Laida, 'they'll eventually disappear.' It is difficult to establish new mangrove plantations; crabs and shellfish damage the seedlings, and even well-rooted young plants can be destroyed by monsoon winds. Replanting is a labour-intensive operation

below Mangrove forest. Once, such forests lined much of the coast, but vast areas of mangroves have been destroyed, often to make way for commercial prawn farms.

Nonoy Regalado/ Oxfam

requiring genuine community involvement if it is to be successful.

A number of income-generating projects have also been established, the most important of which involves ecotourism. In 1995 five cottages, a staff house, a kitchen and dining hall were built on a small island which can only be reached by boat or by a long walk on raised platforms through a mangrove forest. During the first year well over a thousand visitors were received at the centre. Many were school children who had come on day visits to learn about the marine wildlife. Although a long way off the tourist track, and difficult to reach, the bay's natural beauty attracts local and foreign tourists, who are charged a modest fee for food, accommodation and boat hire. Visitors who do not use public transport must pay an extra 25 per cent as a 'carbon tax'.

The project has some way to go before it can be considered an unmitigated success. Dynamite fishing and other destructive techniques are still used by some in the waters outside the wetland park, and the new system of mangrove management is in its infancy. However, much has been achieved during a short time: fish stocks have increased; a competent and dedicated team of local people now manages the park; education programmes have convinced the vast majority of fishers that their future depends on sound and sustainable management. According to Pipuli's community organiser, Billy Marata, approximately half of the fishers were opposed to the sanctuary when it was first mooted. Now very few are not supportive. Community-based coastal resource management may be a dreary-sounding mouthful, but it is evidently an idea whose time has come.

above Baliangao wetland park, a successful community initiative.

left Billy Marata, Pipuli community organiser, inspecting newly-planted mangrove seedlings.

Nonoy Regalado/ Oxfam

above Fishing boats on Taal Lake.

Fishers in search of a fair deal

The First Fisherfolk Unity Congress should have been held in December 1989, but some of the delegates were caught up on EDSA in the pitched battles which followed an attempted coup. 'We had to delay it for a month,' recalls Delfin Carlos, laughing at the memory. Then in January 1990, 300 fisher leaders turned up at the reconvened congress and we agreed that what we needed most was a new Fisheries Code.' Delfin became the deputy coordinator for NACFAR, the National Coalition of Fisherfolks for Aquatic Reform, and since then he has observed with oscillating emotions of hope and despair the passage of various bills through the House of Representatives and the Senate.

The Philippines has a bicameral system of government similar to the United States. The Senate, the upper house, has 24 members who are elected nationally,

and the House of Representatives has 204 congressmen elected at district level. Legislation must be approved by both houses before it is submitted to the president.

During the Eighth Congress, which ended in 1992 (congressional elections are held every three years, presidential every six), a fisheries bill was introduced. 'The bill was pro-fisherfolk,' explains Delfin Carlos, 'but there were too many key people against it.' Among opponents of the bill was the chairman of the Committee on Food and Agriculture, Pablo Garcia. He and other senators with interests in commercial fishing and aquaculture were opposed to those measures which appeared to favour artisanal fishers. For example, the bill proposed that coastal fisheries should be locally run by resource management councils (RMCs); it also proposed the extension of municipal waters from seven to 15 kilometres, and a moratorium on the conversion of mangrove forests to prawn farms. Garcia and his allies managed to stall the bill's progress and it failed to reach the president by the end of the congress.

'So we were back to square one,' says Delfin Carlos, 'and we had to start lobbying all over again.' During the Ninth Congress (1992-1995) the bill made even slower headway; again, vested interests, especially on the Agriculture Committee and in the House of Representatives, were largely responsible for its lack of progress. However, there were some tangible gains. President Ramos issued an executive order which paved the way for the creation of municipal resource management councils. This, according to Delfin Carlos, though a diluted version of what NACFAR was campaigning for, was a move in the right direction.

Following the failure of the bill to become law during the Ninth Congress, NACFAR decided to change tack. It has subsequently spent less time lobbying senators and congressmen and more in organising mass rallies and campaigning for change through the media.

Social reform?

President Ramos has shown a greater interest in the problems of artisanal fishers than his predecessor, and he has promised that a Fisheries Code will be passed before his presidency ends in 1998. The Fisheries Code is part of Ramos's Social Reform Agenda (SRA), which can be seen as a codicil to *Philippines 2000*. It was clear within a year of its introduction that *Philippines 2000*, the neo-liberal strategy for economic reform, was doing little to help the majority of poor Filipinos. The Social Reform Agenda, which was formalised in 1994, was intended to improve social conditions in areas which were untouched by *Philippines 2000* strategy. Critics point out that it does not involve additional spending, rather a redistribution of the existing budget. The term Social Reform Agenda is also misleading: yes, it does include social reforms — the Fisheries Code, if enacted as the artisanal fishers hope, will be precisely that — but it also finances activities and organisations which can scarcely be considered reformist. For example, 70 per cent of the national police budget is categorised as SRA money.

However, for all his reformist rhetoric, Ramos remains a *trapo* politician. '*Trapo*' is an abbreviation of traditional politics — it also means a dirty rag — and it is used to define a system which relies on patronage, feudalism, and the old boy network. A new Fisheries Code will become law. That much is certain. But *trapo* politicians may still manage to water down proposals which would give local communities, and the fishers themselves, the power and the means to manage their own resources.

The Social Reform Agenda has at least given non-governmental organisations (NGOs) and coalitions such as NACFAR an opportunity to influence government policy and legislation, and these groups are now consulted as a matter of course by the committees responsible for drawing up new legislation.

below Danao Bay CBCRM programme coordinator, Aida Laranjo.

Nonoy Regalado/ Oxfam

Between the devil and the deep blue sea

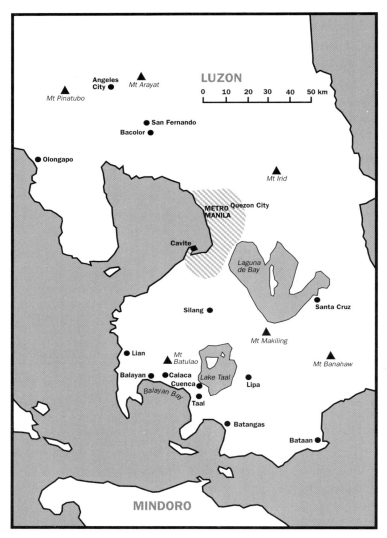

The *Philippines 2000* initiative is described by the government as a 'massive drive for industrialisation', a drive in which foreign investment plays a crucial role. To achieve the goal of NIC (New Industrialised Country) status by 1998, the government has established eight export-oriented 'growth points', or regional industrial centres (RICs). The largest of these, and the flagship of the government's economic policy, is the CALABARZON, an acronym which combines the names of the five participating provinces: Cavite, Laguna, Batangas, Rizal and Quezon. The provinces lie to the south of Manila and they encompass a mixture of prime farmland and spectacular uplands, major lakes such as Taal and Laguna, and a lengthy coastline which is densely studded with fishing villages. The government is encouraging industrial development in the RICs by financing large scale infra-structure projects and by providing incentives for domestic and foreign investors.

The small market town of Calaca occupies an area of flattish land to the north of Balayan Bay. The road into town goes under a white arch which is painted with golden letters that read: CALACA 2000 — Investment Paradise. IT'S RIGHT IN BATANGAS. The town itself is a sleepy backwater and shows little evidence of recent investment, but the government's export-oriented policies are already changing the face of the surrounding countryside. New industrial complexes are being constructed on the coastal farmland, together with roads and factories. However, for many

left Tessie Lopez (left) at a meeting of the women fishers' association in Palikpikan. CERD is helping fishing communities fighting eviction.

communities it will be paradise lost, not found: scores of fishing families in villages near Calaca are threatened with eviction as a result of the new developments.

The dispossessed

Among the largest of the 36 new industrial developments in Batangas will be a power plant at Calaca and an aluminium smelting plant which is being developed by Bacnotan Consolidated Industries. Land prices in the Calaca area have rocketed. In 1990 a square metre of land cost 75 pesos or less; now land fetches between 300 and 400 pesos a square metre. Local elites have success-fully speculated on the rising price of land, buying it when it was less than 100 pesos a square metre and selling it for 300 pesos or more.

The 20 or so members of the women fishers' association in Palikpikan frequently meet in the tiny, open-sided church at the heart of their village; there they discuss their problems and draw up plans to improve their standard of living. In the early years the association was primarily concerned with problems of poverty, ill health, and so on. The women set up a credit scheme and many have taken out low-interest loans to establish small businesses, such as fish-vending and pig-rearing. They have also taken on responsibility for cleaning the sandy streets, which are prettily lined with flowering shrubs, and, more recently, for evaluating the threat posed by industrial development.

In 1995 a plot of land beside the fishers' dwellings was sold to Makati-Agro, which intends to build grain silos, warehouses, and a small port facility. Soon after the site was sold, the women heard that a powerful local landowning family was claiming ownership of the land where they lived. 'We always thought that this land was government property,' explains Tessie Lopez, 'but now we've been told that a member of that family is claiming it.' Her husband, who died recently, was formerly the *barangay* captain, and unlike many village women, Tessie has the confidence to tackle municipal officials. When she investigated the claim to the land occupied by the fishers she found that the land was untitled. However, the family had made a tax declaration for the land in preparation for claiming the title.

above Alberto Marcial, whose family has lived in Salong for over a century.

'The mayor has told us that many people are coming here looking for land,' says Tessie. 'and we fear that we'll be evicted.'

In Salong, a short distance down the coast, 31 families received eviction notices in 1995. They occupy 18 hectares of land between the cane fields and the beach where they keep their *bancas*, and until recently they believed it was theirs. 'I'll get straight to the point,' says Alberto Marcial, a rugged-featured old man with close-cropped grey hair. 'Our major problem is ignorance of the law. Our families never bought this land, but my ancestors have been here for over 100 years. I thought we owned it. Now we find that someone applied for the title in 1970.'

Feudal landlords are well aware of how to use the law to their advantage. They do not even need to buy the land, but simply to lay claim to it. In 1994 the local landowner who had applied for the land-title approached the fishers and offered to sell them the land, at 370 pesos a square metre. 'Before it was worth maybe 75 pesos,' says Alberto, 'but we couldn't even have afforded that.' The fishing families offered 50 pesos a square metre, to be paid over a period of time. This offer was rejected. The fishers expect to be evicted and they assume that the land will be sold to Bacnotan Consolidated Industries.

Fighting the evictions

When the 31 families received the eviction notices they decided to contest them in the courts, and the Department of Justice provided them with a public attorney. The petitioners soon realised that the attorney was doing little to further their case; indeed he even signed an affidavit which stated that they accepted that they resided in an area owned by the man who had laid claim to it. They dismissed their attorney, who is now representing the opposition, and the case has subsequently been handled by a lawyer provided by CERD (Community Extension for Research and Development). 'A pity CERD wasn't here 30 years ago,' says one of the women wistfully. 'If they had been, that man wouldn't have got the title.' Possibly not.

CERD's programme co-ordinator in Batangas is Carlos Flores, a young man with a pragmatic understanding of the feudal politics which govern rural society. He doubts whether his organisation, which has pioneered community-based coastal resources management programmes in Batangas and Samar, will be able to save the fishers of Salong from eviction. 'And there is nothing we can do to stop the process of industrialisation,' he admits. 'But we can demand things from government. If we can delay industrial schemes or land sales and evictions by using the courts, that will cost government and industry money. I think they will be forced to take note of us and of the fishing communities who are suffering.'

It is sometimes said that there is little wrong with the environmental laws in the Philippines; rather, it is their application that leaves much to be desired. The enforcement agencies are under-funded and under-staffed, and a combination of *trapo* politics and corruption means that many illegal practices — from dynamite fishing to illegal trawling, from logging in protected areas to polluting almost everywhere — continue to degrade the environment. In the rush to develop, government agencies and local politicians frequently ignore environmental protection laws.

All industrial developments, in law, should be subject to an Environmental Impact Analysis (EIA), carried out by the Department of Environment and Natural Resources, and should not proceed until DENR awards an Environmental Compliance Certificate (ECC). No EIA has been carried out on Bacnotan's smelting plant, no ECC has been granted, yet the development is going ahead. None of which will bother those municipal officials and corporate interests who stand to profit from the development, whether through local taxes or commercial spin-offs. When the municipality arranged hearings to discuss the Bacnotan development, organisations such as those founded by the fishers of Salong and Palikpikan were not invited.

According to Carlos Flores, central government has no programmes for the resettlement of evacuated communities. It assumes that the municipalities will deal with the problem. 'We accept that some people will be displaced,' says Flores, 'but development should not go ahead unless there is an adequate resettlement programme in place.'

Flores estimates that at least 6,000 people are facing eviction in Batangas to make way for CALABARZON developments. Around 5,000 alone are being displaced for the Cavite-Batangas highway, and smaller numbers are likely to be evicted in dozens of other sites. Throughout the country *Philippines 2000* is proving to be nothing more than an eviction notice for many poor communities. What makes this unacceptable is not so much the fact of eviction — development is always likely to be accompanied by displacement — as the government's steadfast refusal to recognise that it has obligations. If families are to be evicted, they must be resettled, and resettled in a manner which enables them to continue to make a living, be they fishers, farmers, or rag-pickers.

left People are displaced by large-scale agricultural as well as industrial development. Temporary huts by the roadside house people whose land was taken over for palm-oil plantations.

Trouble on the lake

Nonoy Regalado / Oxfam

Laguna Lake, the largest freshwater body in the Philippines, is slowly dying. Bordering on Metro Manila, it has been used for decades as a repository for industrial waste. A government survey in 1979 declared that 90 per cent of the 424 industrial establishments on the shore were 'highly pollutive'. By then another factor was also threatening the lake's ecosystem: fish-pen culture, which began in the early 1970s. By 1983 there were 1,034 pens covering 34,000 hectares, or 40 per cent of the lake. That year seven fishermen were killed in the escalating conflict between the fish-pen owners, who employed armed guards, and the traditional fishers, whose share of the catch had plummeted. Not only were the fish-pens depriving them of water they once fished, they had increased competition among the fish for the lake's food resources. As a result of industrial pollution and fish culture 23 species of fish have become extinct in the lake.

To the south of Laguna is Taal Lake. Roughly oval in shape with an island volcano, still active, at its heart, Taal is one of the most beautiful sights in southern Luzon. Its north and eastern shores are in places densely populated and easy of access — 70,000 people live in the ten municipalities around the lake — while many of the villages in the south are well off the beaten track and unaffected by industrial or other developments.

To reach Don Juan you must either take a *banca* from San Nicolas, on the other side of the lake, or make the knee-wobbling descent down 1500 stone steps that zigzag through the orchards and palm groves which clothe the lower flanks of Mount Maculot. The fortunate visitor may be invited to eat *tawiles*, one of 25 species of fish endemic to Taal, in the shade of the mango trees at the water's edge.

Don Juan has a population of 3,000 and the breadwinners in most families make a living as gill-net and hook-and-line fishers. Some supplement their income by working in the orchards and palm groves. The story the fishers have to tell is little different from the one you hear on the coast. 'In the 1970s,' explains Virgilio Roxas over a lunch of *tawiles* and fruit, 'we used to catch at least 15 kilos of milkfish on each trip. Now we get between one and five kilos at the most.'

The reasons for the declining catch are various. Purse-seiners, motorised push-netters and ring-netters have been partly responsible. These three forms of fishing are far more efficient, in terms of hauling fish out of the water, than the traditional methods used by artisanal fishers, who either use a hook and line or small gill-nets. Purse- seiners, in contrast, employ massive nets which are set and hauled by trawlers; in one night a purse-seiner can catch as many fish as a gill-netter will in a month. Ring-netting and push-netting also involve a capital-intensive approach, although both require more manpower than purse-seining.

Fish-pens have also affected the catch of artisanal fishers. Most are sited at the mouth of the Pancipit River, which flows towards Balayan Bay. According to the artisanal fishers, the use of artificial feed in the pens has led to eutrophication: the nutrient input increases algal growth, which causes a decrease in oxygen, especially in still water. The use of pesticides in the fish-pens is also thought to be harmful. 'We don't like fish culture,' says Mrs Milagros Chavez, president of KMMLT, the lake's organisation of fishers. 'We don't want Taal Lake to go the same way as Laguna.' Besides the polluting effects of fish culture, she fears that the pens in the Pancipit River are hindering the passage of migratory fish.

The fishers of Don Juan speak scathingly of those who control the commercial fisheries in the lake. Over half the fish-pen owners, they say, are outsiders from Manila and elsewhere who care little for the lake's long-term future. Many are military officers and politicians and they have used their influence to circumvent laws which are supposed to regulate their activities.

A quarter of an hour by *banca* from Don Juan is the village of Lunang Lipa. According to Nelson Manalo, a *barangay* councillor and a ring-net owner, life for the villagers is full of hardship.

The ring-netters do at least provide work, says Nelson Manalo. It takes 100 people to operate the nets and profits from the catch, which might be as high as 100 gallons of fish a night, are divided between the owner, the boatmen, the pushers, and the lamp-holders, each taking a quarter.

'You can't stop people making a living,' explains Nelson. 'We have no land, no jobs — all we can do is fish. If ring-net fishing was banned, we'd have no livelihood.'

In the next village, an articulate old man rails against all forms of commercial fishing in the lake. He says that the government makes laws, but fails to enforce them as the people who own the purse-seiners and the push-nets have friends and relatives in high places. 'What we need is a revolution,' he suggests. 'We need a new system. The whole country depends on peasants and fishers for food.'

The artisanal fishers of Lake Taal are also worried about the impact of CALABARZON projects. Industrial development, water extraction, road improvements, and new tourist sites may all affect the lake's ecology over the coming years. Some municipalities see tourism as the best way of generating wealth and jobs. However, the fishers are less enthusiastic. Midway through 1996 they heard rumours that an American consortium was planning to build a golf-course on land which had been acquired by a Taiwanese company and that several families faced eviction. Lack of information is a perennial problem in the Philippines; it is hard for people affected by development plans to challenge those plans when developers and government agencies fail to supply them with detailed information.

Pushed to the limits

above This family in New Paco have a small-holding on which they grow a variety of vegetables, and keep a few animals.

right Tahalyong Sulayman, *datu* of New Paco village. In his lifetime, he has watched the forests of the Arakan Valley being destroyed.

Badang Layoran is the *datu* of Bagtok village. 'When the settlers first came here,' he explains, 'our ancestors welcomed them. They even gave them land.' Badang's people, the Manobo of Mindanao, were later to realise that such largesse — with plots of land being exchanged for tins of fish and bags of rice — was a mistake. 'Yes,' muses Badang, 'we were fooled by the settlers. But we've learned our lesson — the land we have now will remain ours. We can't move again, and besides there's nowhere else to go.'

Several hours' walk from Bagtok, perched on a hillside with spectacular views of the Arakan Valley, is the settlement of Paco-paco. Its *datu*, Tahalyong Sulayman, has a similar story to tell. Encompassing with a sweep of the arms the great bowl of largely treeless land below the village, he says: 'When I was a child all this was thick forest. A lot of lowlanders say that it was our slash-and-burn farming that did this. It wasn't. The settlers started it, and the logging companies did the rest.' A generation ago the Manobo were the sole occupants of the 70,000-hectare Arakan Valley; today all but 10-15,000 hectares is in the possession of non-tribal settlers, and much of the rest has been degraded by logging.

Paco-paco is picturesque and poor. Ten families, most with seven or more children, live in a scattering of thatched bamboo huts. The huts are spotlessly clean and tidy. Families sleep together in one room and cook and eat in the other. Pigs and poultry search for pickings around the huts, and in the fields beyond grow maize, sweet potato, cassava, and gabi. Having lost so much of their land, the Manobo have been forced to change their farming methods: the fields are now continuously tilled and in places the soils are becoming exhausted.

Paco-paco has no electricity or piped water, and the nearest school and health clinic are many miles away. However, the modern world is impinging on their lives: they listen to American pop music on the radio and there is a netball hoop where the young play outside the *datu*'s hut. The wealthier among them buy fertiliser and pesticides to put on their fields, and goods such as shag tobacco — which they roll in old newspaper — and kerosene lamps are found in many homes.

According to *datu* Tahalyan, his people were better off in the days before the settlers and loggers came. 'We were never hungry when I was a child,' he recalls. 'There was always food in the forest. Now we've joined a new sort of economy. We can go to stores and buy things, but you need money for that.'

Datu Badazng of Bagtok agrees. 'Before we had no money. Now we have — sometimes — but we're worse off. The people in the lowlands buy our produce at a low price, but they sell their own goods at a high price, so we can't afford them.'

However, both leaders add that the situation has begun to improve. They have discovered allies in the lowlands and they have begun to assert themselves politically. With the help of a theatre group and a church-based organisation, the Manobos are uniting to save their land and culture.

A people under siege

An estimated 4.5 million Filipinos belong to what are variously described as indigenous cultural communities, hill tribes, ethnic minorities or indigenous peoples, the latter being the preferred term now. Forty separate ethnolinguistic groups fall into six major categories. The largest, with over 2.1 million individuals and 18 ethnolinguistic groups, are the lumads of Mindanao. The second most populous group, with a million members, comprises the indigenous people of the Cordillera, the mountainous backbone of northern Luzon. The remaining groups have between 110,000 and 160,000 members each. These comprise the tribes which inhabit the Caraballo mountain range in east-central Luzon; the Mangyan of Mindoro; the hill tribes of Palawan; and the Aeta and Agta, who are widely distributed throughout the Philippines. A further 13 ethnolinguistic groups in Mindanao are collectively known as the Moro, which is Spanish for Moor. Although classified by the government as an indigenous cultural community, the Moro's bonds of communality relate more to their religion, Islam, than their race.

Three and a half centuries of Spanish occupation brought 85 per cent of the population into the Christian fold. The remainder consisted of the Moros, who

left Arakan Valley, once thickly forested.

actively fought against the Spanish, and the indigenous peoples, who avoided them by retreating from the colonial spheres of influence. There were a few exceptions. By the 1890s there were some 200,000 Christians in Mindanao, most being lumads, but by and large the isolation of the area ensured that indigenous peoples retained their language, folklore, and religion.

During the past century all but the remotest regions have been brought into some form of contact with the modern world. The Manobo of Arakan Valley were first visited by government officials in the 1930s at a time when the Americans were exploring the interior of Mindanao. The first US governor-general in Mindanao had declared: 'It is difficult to imagine a richer country or one out of which more can be made than the island of Mindanao.' Areas which had never been penetrated by the Spanish were now rapidly opened up and an influx of settlers — most being landless peasants from the overcrowded Visayas — came to grab a slice of the promised land. The province of Cotabato — now subdivided into five smaller provinces — is typical of the island as a whole. In 1918 there were 172,000 people living in 36 municipalities.

By 1970 the population had risen to 1.6 million, having increased ten-fold in just over 50 years, largely as a result of the resettlement policy of the government.

When the settlers arrived in the Arakan Valley they brought with them ideas and customs which were alien to the Manobo. Most significantly, they saw land as a commodity which could be bought, sold and used for financial gain as well as subsistence. The settlers gradually took over the lower-lying land and the Manobo retreated further into the forest. The peace they found was short-lived. *Datu* Badong Layolan vividly recalls the arrival of commercial loggers. 'They used guards to drive us out,' he recalls, 'and if we refused to go they simply cut the trees around our huts, so people had to flee to save themselves.'

By the late 1970s, over 150 local companies had been granted logging concessions covering 5 million hectares of Mindanao. These encompassed most of the lumads' territory and were awarded without consideration to either their needs, or to the problems which inevitably resulted from the destruction of the forests. At the turn of the century most of Mindanao was clothed in trees; less than 18 per cent is under forest cover now. Commercial logging, illegal in most areas, continues with the connivance of government officials. By the late 1970s most of Arakan's forests had been logged out, but one company continued to operate illegally as recently as 1991. The battle to expel the loggers signalled the beginning of a new era for the Manobo.

The Manobo fight back

Father Fausto Tentorio does not look like a priest. He wears a t-shirt, shorts and a collection of bead bracelets, one of which bears the nickname the Manobo have given him: Pops. A member of the Italian order PIME, the Pontifical Institute for Foreign Mission, he is based at Greenfields, a town at the heart of a 'green revolution' agricultural scheme in the Arakan Valley.

below Father Fausto Tentorio, of PIME.

Nonoy Regalado/ Oxfam

When he arrived in 1990 he and a colleague visited the Manobo in Bagtok and the hills beyond. 'They immediately told us about the problem they had with the loggers,' recalls Father Fausto. A timber company was operating in the forests on the Manobo's sacred mountain, Mount Sinaka, and the Manobo asked the priest to help them stop the logging. 'The Department of Environment and Natural Resources agreed that they shouldn't be logging,' explains Father Fausto. 'They came and confiscated the bulldozer for a while, but as soon as the officials left, the logging began again.' Then in 1991 the Manobo hijacked the bulldozer and barricaded the site for three weeks. The loggers eventually withdrew.

'After that,' explains Father Fausto, 'the Manobo began to visit us regularly and tell us about their problems, and we realised that if we were to help them we needed an identity outside the church.' The Tribal Filipino Programme for Community Development Incorporated (TFPCDI) was founded in 1992. In the villages TFPCDI has helped set up sustainable agriculture schemes and introduced primary health care and literacy programmes. It was also instrumental in establishing MALUPA, a people's organisation with 18 local chapters. MALUPA has successfully claimed over 5,000 hectares of land as ancestral domain.

'MALUPA has given us hope,' says *datu* Tahalyong bluntly. 'Now we have ancestral domain certificates from the government, so we feel more secure, and we've set up a committee to determine how we should manage our land.' Paco-paco's committee, or *salihanan*, is introducing laws — or at least, codes of behaviour — which all must abide by. It will not allow any Visayan settlers to occupy land within its ancestral domain; it has also banned public consumption of alcohol, and gambling. When Father Fausto first visited the people of Bagtok

Nonoy Regalado/ Oxfam

and Paco-paco in 1991, they were selling land for as little as 1,000 pesos (£20) a hectare. Now, he says, they hardly ever sell land to outsiders: 'They realise that if they're to have a future, it will be based on their land.'

It is the duty of the municipal government to provide essential public services, but when people of Paco-paco have asked the authorities to provide schools and health care facilities, they always say the same thing, complains one of the villagers. 'They say "But you've got that priest Fausto, so why don't you ask him to help you?" And then they turn us away.'

above TFPCDI organises a literacy programme and primary health care initiative among the Manobo in the Arakan valley: (above) literacy class, with a teacher who is married to a Manobo man; (below) Jasmin Badilla, a community health worker, visiting a mother in Bagtok, walks many miles to reach isolated settlements.

God, nature and other practical matters

above Mandialay Bagsilanon, a healer who uses traditional methods to treat illnesses.

Mandialay Bagsilanon is a healer. A small, wiry man with a wispy beard, he arrives at the bamboo hut where guests stay in Bagtok in an ornately embroidered waistcoat and a tassled head-dress. 'When I'm trying to heal,' he says 'I always ask for the help of Manama, the supreme creator.' According to Manobo mythology, Manama created two rivers, the Pulangi and the Agusan, to help to balance the earth and prevent it swaying during earthquakes. Manama oversees the spirits which reside throughout nature, in rocks, trees, rivers, and mountains. With Manama's help, Mandialay says he can see which part of the body is suffering from illness. 'It's as though a light is shining,' he explains, 'and when I see where the sickness is, I can suck it out.'

When Christian missionaries first encountered the Manobo they told them that worship of Manama was evil, and many of the evangelical groups which have recently arrived in Mindanao continue to press this view. They have sought not only to undermine the traditional beliefs of the Manobo, but their self-worth as well. Manobos who become evangelical pastors are forbidden from preaching in their own language; instead they have been made to use Visayan, the language of the settlers. According to Father Fausto Tentorio, this reinforces the idea that the Manobo are inferior to the settlers, that God does not speak their language.

Father Fausto's order, PIME, was founded in the nineteenth century to work among and convert non-Christians. Today conversion is no longer seen as part of their mission in Mindanao. 'What we must realise,' explains the priest, 'is that the Manobo's religion is the religion of life. Theirs is a god who can be seen everywhere in nature.' Traditionally, at the time of planting and harvesting, the Manobo say a *panubad*, a prayer to Manama. Father Fausto found that the practice was beginning to die out when he first arrived, but over the past years he has noticed that the Manobo, keen to assert their cultural identity, are once again observing the old religious ceremonies.

There are times when the traditional healers do more than summon Manama's help. Mandialay uses herbs to cure certain ailments: *alibangbang* for backache, for example, and *pula-pula* for sore eyes. When he was young such herbs were plentiful in the forests surrounding the village. Nowadays, the only untouched forest with a good supply of herbs is on the flanks of Mount Sinaka, which is many hours' walk away. The loss of forest has affected every aspect of Manobo life.

Medicinal herbs are scarcer, and so are the monkeys and other creatures which once formed an important part of the Manobo diet. But these are relatively minor matters when seen in the light of the agricultural changes which have been forced on the Manobo by loss of land and deforestation.

In the remoter parts of the Philippines indigenous communities still practice *kaingin*. A plot of land is cleared of trees and planted with crops. After harvest, the land is left fallow for several years, during which time the soil's fertility is naturally replenished. In the meantime the farmers make use of plots elsewhere, hence the term 'shifting cultivation'. The practice is sustainable and environmentally benign providing there is no shortage of land. For most of the Manobo of Arakan, however, *kaingin* is a thing of the past. Having lost most of

their land and forest, they have been forced to cultivate their land on a continuous basis.

To help the Manobo to adapt to settled farming, DKTFP has established over 70 separate projects. At Bagtok, Gory Paron, a young agronomist, is teaching villagers SALT, or Sloping Agricultural Land Technology, on the hillside above the village. 'Our main aim,' he explains as he watches a score of villagers weeding, 'is to control soil erosion by reducing tillage and to keep fertility high through crop rotation and the use of natural fertilisers.' The four-hectare plot consists of ribbons of crops divided by rows of fruit trees, planted at 20 metre intervals. The land is neither ploughed nor harrowed and crops are rotated, with rice being followed by ground nuts, legumes, corn, and a rootcrop. The fruit trees are linked by a nitrogen-fixing hedge, which binds

below Crop rotation and the use of natural fertilisers can help to reduce soil erosion on steep slopes. Villagers weed a plot set up by TFPCDI to teach the methods of Sloping Agricultural Land Technology. The weeds are used as a mulch to conserve water and enrich the soil.

right Gory Paron of TFPCDI and the village *datu* examining mango, rattan, and mahogany seedlings in the tree nursery in Bagtok village.

the soil and whose clippings are used as a weed-suppressing mulch. Instead of using the high-yielding varieties of rice favoured by the settlers in the lowlands, the Manobo plant traditional strains which show better resistance to pests and diseases. The village *salihanan* has worked out a schedule which ensures that every family is involved in the weeding, sowing, harvesting, and general management of the crops.

DKTFP has also helped villagers in the Arakan Valley to establish tree nurseries and such species as mango, rattan, and mahogany are now being planted on both private and communal plots of land. Another programme has enabled Manobo villagers to acquire *carabao*, or water buffalo, which provide milk and draught power to plough the flatter land. The beneficiaries of this scheme are given interest-free loans which are repayable after three years.

In some villages, Manobo have taken out loans to buy pigs and goats; in others DKTFP has established herb gardens, and this means that healers like Mandialay Bagsilanon no longer have to make the long trek to Mount Sinaka.

Hardly any Manobo children attend government schools and only one in ten adult Manobos can read and write. Father Fausto believes that basic education can do much to help the indigenous peoples. By this he means not only literacy training, which is proving popular among the women, but education in primary health care. 'It took us two years to convince the people in Bagtok that many of the diseases were the result of poor sanitation and that they needed to do something about it,' he recalls. In 1995 the villagers constructed two communal toilets, and the incidence of diarrhoea has fallen.

Claiming the land

left Manobo women and children, New Paco.

A Manobo goes into Mount Apo national park and is accosted by a monkey. The monkey says: 'Hey! You can't come in here.' The Manobo replies: 'But I'm an indigenous person!' 'Yes, I know that,' says the monkey impatiently, 'but you shouldn't be here. Only we animals have rights here.'

In some instances indigenous people do have the right to live in national parks, but this story, told by a Manobo of Paco-paco, illustrates the insecurity which many feel about their land. Having been driven further and further into the hills, they are now eager to protect and reserve for themselves the land which they still occupy. In an ideal world, they would be given titles to their ancestral domain, conferring rights of ownership.

So far the state has refused to grant freehold titles; instead it has introduced measures to enable indigenous peoples to claim occupation but not ownership of their homelands.

Under the 1987 constitution, all mineral and forest lands, public parks and reservations, and land which the government has yet to classify belong to the state, which, as a result, owns 53 per cent of the Philippine land mass. 'Forest land' is defined as all land with a slope of 18 per cent or more, regardless of whether or not it is forested. The vast majority of indigenous people consequently find themselves on land which is owned by the state, responsibility for whose management is primarily vested in the Department of Environment and Natural

Resources (DENR). The constitution recognised the existence of ancestral domains, but the state retained the right of ownership and control. However, in 1993, in response to the long-standing calls for the recognition of indigenous land rights, DENR administrative order 02 (DA 02) provided for the identification and delineation of ancestral domains.

Indigenous people can now apply to DENR for Certificates of Ancestral Domain Claims, or CADCs. They must provide maps showing the boundaries to their claim, together with a detailed history of their occupation of the land. They cannot claim land which they have lost to settlers or others in the past. So far three million hectares — ten per cent of the country — has been subject to claims for CADCs, and DENR has approved them for a quarter of this area.

According to Professor Marvic Leonen, director of the Legal Rights and National Resources Centre (LRC) in Manila, DENR is only approving claims for land where there is no sign of commercial opposition:

'When mining companies or ranches have their eyes on the land,' says Professor Leonen, 'then DENR is not giving the CADCs'. Frequently, applications are lost in the bureaucratic machinery of government. There are plenty of places to get lost: LRC has calculated that there are 26 separate steps between application and approval. CADCs only provide partial protection against development as they do not give protection against projects which are carried out or sanctioned by other government departments. This means, for example, that a CADC provides protection against forestry plantation, but not a hydro-electric power scheme of the Department of Energy.

In the Arakan Valley MALUPA has successfully claimed 5,241 hectares of land as ancestral domain, and 464 families are registered as the beneficiaries of five separate CADCs. A further three claims are still pending with DENR, and as there is no commercial activity in this part of the valley, they will probably be granted. *Datu* Badang Layoran of Bagtok says that they now feel more secure about their situation. 'When we received the certificate,' he recalls, 'we felt we could at last plan for the future.'

A clash of cultures

Some of the indigenous people living in the remote Cordillera have rejected the laws of the state, arguing that they have lived peacefully for centuries with their own system of administration. They remain relatively untouched by the outside world and they possess sufficient land to continue practising terraced rice cultivation and *kaingin* agriculture.

The lumads in Mindanao would like to argue a similar case, but they are in no position to do so. Their homelands are fragmented and they have long been forced to interact with the non-tribal world. The clash of cultures is now as pronounced as it has ever been, and people like the B'laan of southern

right Father Peter Geremiah of DKTFP. An outspoken champion of the poor and dispossessed, he is detested by those in power, and has twice been imprisoned on trumped-up charges.

Nonoy Regalado / Oxfam

Mindanao are threatening to take up arms if their lands suffer further encroachment. Unlike the Manobo of Arakan Valley, the B'laan live on land which may well be rich in minerals.

Half a century ago the B'laan occupied a vast area of valleys and hills around the town of Columbio. Since then they have lost much of it. In 1950 two presidential proclamations set aside 30,000 hectares for rice and corn production; this was classified as a resettlement site and migrants flowed in from the Visayas. Timber-licence agreements led to the felling of most of the forest land around Columbio, and pasture leases allowed ranchers to convert the logged areas into grassland. Another wave of settlers arrived in the 1960s, and the B'laan retreated further into the hills when armed conflict flared up between Muslim separatists and government forces in the 1970s. Since then there have been many killings, of innocents caught in the crossfire and of tribal leaders who refused to leave land coveted by the Muslims. In 1993 11 B'laan were massacred in the village of Lampiras. When asked who the killers were, Father Peter Geremiah of the Diocese of Kidapwan Tribal Filipino Programme (DKTFP) admitted that no-one knew for sure. Muslim separatists, Christian fanatics, local politicians and cattle ranchers had all been implicated in killings over the past 20 years. The B'laan were frequently the victims, though being a warrior tribe they were not averse to settling old scores.

The B'laan now constitute 30 per cent of the population of Columbio district, the Muslims 20 per cent and the settlers the rest. According to Father Peter, the lack of land security — stemming partly from the conflicting claims of the three communities and partly from the threat now posed by a mining company — is the principal factor underlying the conflicts in the area.

above Land congress, where B'laan and government officials met to discuss indigenous land rights.

With the help of DKTFP the B'laan established La Bugal Tribal Council, the counterpart to the Manobo's MALUPA. In 1988 it successfully petitioned the government to cancel timber and pasture licences granted to a large ranching company, and it subsequently spearheaded the campaign for the recognition of B'laan ancestral domains. In 1993 the B'laan made claims to 21,400 hectares. Unfortunately, some of this lay within the resettlement area established in 1950 and responsibility for its management rests with the Department of Agrarian Reform (DAR), not DENR. Under the government's land reform programme DAR can grant Certificates of Land Ownership Awards (CLOAs). These were conceived as a means of providing land to landless farmers and they are limited to three hectares per family. The B'laan argued that they should be granted collective ownership of their CLOAs, and that the 3-hectare limit per family should not apply to them, and DAR has accepted their demand. However, many B'laan are unsatisfied. They claim that settlers have received CLOAs within B'laan territory and that the names of some B'laan families have been missed off the list. They also argue that the collective CLOAs are far too small, and fail to encompass their ancestral domain.

In June 1996 the theatre company Kaliwat organised a Land Congress. At the congress over 50 B'laan from Columbio district met officials from DAR and DENR. Communication was difficult. This was not so much a question of language — most spoke or understood Visayan — as attitude and philosophy. The government officials clearly saw land as a commodity, just as the settlers did. The B'laan, in contrast, talked of land in almost mystical terms: not only did it provide sustenance and most of the necessities of life, it was the abode of Manama and spirits. It was not something which could be parcelled off in plots and exchanged for goods and cash; in short, it could not be owned. But if the government officials failed to understand the B'laan's complex attitude towards land, the B'laan failed to see that the government officials had to work within the constraints of their departments.

When the day-long congress broke up participants seemed moderately satisfied. The B'laan had expressed their fears and anger to the government; the government officials said that they now understood the B'laan's case better; and Kaliwat staff considered it something of a triumph that the two parties had met at all.

Many of the indigenous people in the Philippines fear that they will eventually lose their land. This is often a general apprehension, based on past experience of settlers and loggers. For the B'laan, however, their fears have a sharper focus. In 1995 Western Mining Corporation (WMC) was given permission to prospect for gold and other minerals over an area of almost 100,000 hectares in southern Mindanao. Welcomed by some, reviled by others, WMC may do more to change the way of life in Columbio district than the loggers and settlers ever did. Whether it will be a change for the better or worse is far from certain.

below family working on their land, Arakan valley. Indigenous people regard land in mystical terms as being the abode of spirits.

Nonoy Regalado/ Oxfam

The mining dilemma

An Ancestral Domains Bill made its first appearance in the legislature in 1988, but its passage towards the statute books has been continually thwarted by politicians antipathetic to the cause of the indigenous people. The mining community, in contrast, has suffered no such set-backs. In 1995 the Mining Code paved the way for a new phase in mineral exploitation, with foreign corporations being given special incentives to operate in the country. The government sees mineral exploitation as a way of raising some of the substantial revenue needed to build a modern economy. Foreign corporations possessing the capital and expertise which local mining companies lack are therefore being welcomed into the Philippines.

The Mining Code allows foreign corporations to apply for Financial and Technical Assistance Agreements (FTAAs) which give them the right to explore, develop, and use mineral resources, and auxiliary rights to exploit timber and water. Under the new code, foreign corporations can repatriate all profits once taxes and royalties have been paid to the government.

By June 1996, 67 applications for FTAAs had been filed by mining corporations, covering over a third of the uplands of the Philippines. If one adds to this the 300 or so applications under previous legislation, 67 per cent of the uplands and 42 per cent of the total land area are subject to some form of mineral exploitation claim. While environmental groups stress the enormity of this figure, the mining world is quick to point out that by September 1996 the government had

Nonoy Regalado/ Oxfam

above Linda Datumanong and her family. She believes that without land, her children have no future.

granted only two FTAAs. Both had gone to Australian companies: one to ARIMCO and the other to Western Mining Corporation (WMC), whose Columbio FTAA gives it an exclusive concession for mineral exploitation over 99,400 hectares of land, most of which is considered by the B'laan to be theirs. WMC has three other applications pending. If they are granted, its area of exploration around Columbio will be increased to 400,000 hectares.

There is a presumption, both by WMC and by those who oppose its presence, that the corporation will strike gold and copper in the Colombio FTAA. WMC estimates an 'expected yield of approximately $2,700 million and about $500 million for [the Philippine] government through taxes and fees'. WMC has done its utmost to convince the local population that it will be sensitive both to their needs and to the environment. It intends to operate a preferential employment programme for local people, providing they have the necessary skills; it has established a school for B'laan children where no school existed before, and it has built roads and provided a water supply.

Professor Leonen of LRC agrees that WMC has provided social services which benefit some B'laan, but he believes that these will pale into insignificance when seen in the light of the environmental and social change which mining will cause. 'A huge operation such as this,' he says, 'will shift sovereignty away from the local government, which is responsible for providing services, to the corporation itself. The local government will rely increasingly on mining taxes and this will create serious dilemmas when it comes to balancing the needs of the local people with the demands of the corporation.'

Father Peter Geremiah is more forthright. 'There are some B'laan who are saying, "Yes, we favour WMC, it's building schools and helping us." But that's the government's responsibility,

not a foreign company's! And WMC is using bribery to win people round.'

WMC is now paying salaries to some of the B'laan leaders and giving financial support to tribal councils. While opponents describe this as bribery; WMC sees it as sensible business practice. Some of those who have been approached by WMC with offers of jobs and money have resisted the overtures. These include a Davao City journalist who has written unfavourably about WMC, the director of Kaliwat, and prominent B'laan like Linda Datumanong of Lampiras village. 'I met Mrs X of WMC,' she recalls, 'and she tried to bribe me by giving me a job with a 4,000 peso salary. I refused to sign the contract she had drawn up. I didn't sign it because I am concerned for my children.' She adds that if WMC strikes a commercially viable deposit in or around Lampiras her people will lose some of their land; without land her children have no future.

WMC vows that it will observe the environmental standards which are applicable for mining operations in Australia and it points out that its work will be monitored by DENR. It is disingenuous, counter the B'laan, to claim that open-pit mining can be done in an environmentally sensitive manner, and it is naive to imagine that DENR will effectively police WMC's operations. As evidence they cite events of the recent past. In June 1996 three executives of the Marcopper Mining Corporation, two of whom were Australian, were charged with violations of the Water Code and the Philippines Mining Act and with 'reckless imprudence'. Mine tailings had killed off life in a major waterway on Marinduque Island. Fisheries had been destroyed, irrigated land had been deprived of its water source, and toxic materials leaking from the Canadian-owned mine had led to a dramatic rise in illnesses among local people. Environmentalists claim that events such as the Marcopper disaster are commonplace in the Philippines.

However, DENR maintains that the prosecution of the executives is evidence of the hard-line approach it is now taking against polluters. The Philippines, according to Victor Ramos, Secretary of State for the Environment, is set to become the first 'green tiger' in Asia.

Critics of WMC accuse the corporation of underhand practices and duplicity, but it is clear that some of the company's opponents have wildly exaggerated the impact that its operations are likely to have. The foreign mining lobby could also point out, in its defence, that the small-scale mining operations which are often championed by its critics tend to be far more polluting than large-scale ventures.

The Philippines government is faced by a profound dilemma. If it is to tackle poverty in a lasting way it requires the revenue to create jobs, house people decently, and so forth. There may be better and more benign ways of raising revenue than mining, but one cannot expect a poor country rich in gold and copper to leave its deposits untouched. However, the argument that large-scale mining is in the national interest does not impress the B'laan. The 1950 presidential proclamations which appropriated 30,000 hectares of their land as an agricultural resettlement area were also justified in terms of the national interest, as were numerous logging concessions awarded in the region. None brought any tangible benefits to the B'laan, and most see no reason to suppose that WMC's activities will bring anything other than transitory improvements to their lives.

The B'laan are continuing to press for recognition of their ancestral domain. Whether CADCs will save their land from the bulldozers is a moot point. Professor Leonen is not optimistic. 'If a foreign corporation clashes with indigenous people,' he says, 'it's usually the corporation that wins.'

Asked what her people will do if WMC begins mineral exploitation near her village, Linda Datumanong replies: 'They are still some distance away from Lampiras at the moment. But if they come, we'll be forced to fight back. There will be bloodshed.'

Staging a revival

'When we first went up to the Arakan Valley,' recalls Nestor Horfilla, the director of the Kaliwat Theatre Collective, 'the Manobo had had so many bad experiences with the lowlanders that they feared the worst.' Now, when members of Kaliwat arrive in remote villages like Paco-paco, there are shouts of delight and much embracing and laughter. At first sight the Manobo and the theatre group seem improbable partners — the Manobo are slight of build and reticent by nature; the artistes, as they call themselves, are glamorous, colourful, effervescent — but together they have produced some of the most interesting theatrical work in the Philippines.

left Nestor Horfilla, Director of Kaliwat.

Nonoy Regalado/ Oxfam

above Members of
Kaliwat Theatre Company
in rehearsal. Their plays
are performed throughout
the Philippines, and
elsewhere in the world.
Their plays are more than
entertainment; they carry
an advocacy message,
and encourage audiences
to think about the issues
of land rights and cultural
survival.

Sitting on the steps of a Manobo hut, the vast roadless landscape laid out before him, Richard Belar, one of the original members of Kaliwat, recalls their early experiences: 'In those days we would send a couple of people to a village like this, and they'd spend time here, getting to know the *datu* and his people and asking about their lives, their myths, their history.' With the Manobo's permission, Kaliwat worked up the raw material of research into a play back at their Davao City headquarters. The group then returned to the village and put on a performance. 'We'd work their legends and their dialogue into the piece,' explains Richard, 'and we'd try to tell the story — through dance and music and words — of the people's history and struggles.' Often the Manobo in the audience would get up and complain that something was wrong, or suggest additions. A one-hour piece might take several hours, then afterwards

there would be more discussion about the content.

Kaliwat's members see themselves as technicians whose task it is to present the lumads' stories to the world beyond. Once the Manobo, or whichever of the lumads Kaliwat is working with, approve the play, it goes on tour in theatres, schools, and government offices around the Philippines. In recent years Kaliwat has also performed in Europe, Japan, and Australia. 'Of course, we have to entertain,' says Richard. 'But our plays also have an advocacy role. They explore issues about land, and about the struggles of the lumads and their spirituality, and they encourage the audience to think.'

A new generation of actor/researchers has recently joined Kaliwat. Their various talents — some are musically trained, others can dance and mime — are blended with those of the older members of the collective, but performing takes up less than a third of their time. Much of the rest they spend in the field, often walking for many hours up vertiginous slopes to reach remote villages. 'Our task at the moment,' explained Sheila and Lyndon, whom we meet in Paco-paco, 'is to collect the Manobo's epic stories.' These are then recorded and transformed into comic book form back in Kaliwat's office. The comics are distributed to Mindanao's schools, along with other educational materials, and they help to foster a better understanding among settler children of the lumads' predicament.

People like the Manobo and the B'laan are in a state of transition. They have lost some of their traditions, and they have been forced to adopt the administrative structures imposed by government. The *datu* remain important, but it is the elected *barangay* captains who hold the real power now. The closer they are to the plains, the more indigenous people tend to adopt the settlers' ways of life. According to Father Fausto Tentorio of the Tribal Filipino Programme, the young are more easily lured away from the traditional lifestyle than the old. There is a feeling among them that whatever the settlers have and do must be good, simply because it is modern. This, he says, stems from the lumads' low self-esteem. 'It's very apparent,' says Father Fausto. 'Whenever you have Manobo and settlers meeting in a forum, the Manobo tend to keep quiet. They feel inferior.'

When Kaliwat first visited the Manobo of Arakan Valley they discovered that the art of story-telling was beginning to die out and that it was only the elders who knew the Manobo's myths and tales. Since Kaliwat took an interest, encouraging them not only to share their past, but to participate in performances, the Manobo have realised that their culture is worth preserving. Now, the young people are learning to tell the old stories and to play the traditional lumad instruments.

Theatre has proved to be one of the most effective ways of reaching out to indigenous people, but Kaliwat's work extends far beyond the stage. The collective plays an important role in brokering deals between Mindanao's lumads and the authorities. It has helped them draw up ancestral domain claims and its research has been used to write the supporting histories which DENR requires.

left and below Richard Belar, of Kaliwat, playing a traditional lumad instrument. The theatre group learn the songs and stories of indigenous groups like the Manobo and B'laan.

Living dangerously

Nonoy Regalado / Oxfam

above (top) A wasteland of grey *lahar* covers the fields and villages around Pinatubo in Central Luzon. This is near Bacolor, Pampanga, a once busy and prosperous town, and home to 60,000 people.

above (bottom) Pepe Cuenca beside his new house, built on stilts above his old one which was submerged under a tide of *lahar*.

When Mount Pinatubo erupted in June 1991, spewing 8 billion cubic metres of volcanic debris across Central Luzon, the people of San Juan *barangay* considered themselves fortunate. Over a million people were displaced by the eruption and subsequent mudflows, but San Juan suffered no more than a thick coating of ash and temporary flooding. However, four years later, on 1 October 1995, Typhoon Mameng struck the Philippines and torrential rain turned the volcanic ash into rivers of glutinous *lahar*. San Juan was one of many places buried by this sea of mud. Since the eruption there have been mudflows each *lahar* season — displacing around 800,000 people and killing around 30 people a year — but no-one had foreseen the damage which Typhoon Mameng would wreak. 1.3 million people were displaced and over 430 were killed.

Pepe Cuenca and his extended family — wife, four children, three grandchildren — were asleep in their pleasant home, recently built with the money Pepe had earned during four years in Saudi Arabia, when the mudflows struck. 'I suddenly heard rumbling like galloping horses,' he recalls. 'It was the *lahar*, and it was moving at 60 kilometres an hour by the time it hit San Juan.' Within a quarter of an hour the town had been submerged beneath 15 feet of *lahar*. Pepe and his family climbed onto their tin roof and huddled in the lashing rain, watching the *lahar* rise around their feet. 'For 24 hours,' he recalls with a shudder, 'we had no food, no water, our grandchildren were crying...' Eventually a rescue truck managed to plough across the *lahar* and the family was moved to an evacuation site.

The *lahar* drove four-fifths of San Juan's population, around 1,200 people, into exile: most remain in evacuation camps, staging sites or with relatives elsewhere. Pepe was among those who decided to return, and he now lives with his family in a makeshift hut on stilts, constructed above the roof of his old dwelling. The farmland around his house is a barren waste of grey *lahar* and the church nearby is half-buried. On its walls someone has scrawled *Tumayo ka San Juan*. Rise up San Juan! *Babalik Kaming Muli Ngunit Kailan*. We'll be back, but when?

Many will not be back and it is unlikely that Pepe's hut will survive the next monsoon, even though it is anchored to the ground with anti-typhoon guy ropes. 'Last year,' he says as he scans the barren horizon, 'we lost almost everything.' This is said without rancour or self-pity. He knows that his misfortunes have been shared by millions, not only round Mount Pinatubo, but in many other parts of the Philippines.

The Rim of Fire

The Philippines lies in the Pacific rim of fire. Of its 200 volcanoes, 21 are classified as active although PHIVOLCS, the government institution which studies seismic activity, is only monitoring six of them. Between 1991 and 1995 the cumulative number of people affected by volcanic activity was 3.7 million, most being victims of Pinatubo. The Philippines also lies within the Pacific typhoon belt, and in an average year some 20 typhoons and cyclones batter large parts of the country. Between 1991 and 1995 just under 25 million people were affected by cyclones, generally suffering loss of homes and crops. The entire country with the exception of Palawan province is subject to earthquakes, of which around five a day are recorded.

The Citizens' Disaster Response Centre (CDRC), the leading NGO working in the field, makes a clear distinction between hazards and disasters. A volcanic eruption is a hazard; it only becomes a disaster if it has an impact on the human population. When a cyclone hits a wealthy suburb of Manila it is not, generally speaking, a disaster: the rich live in well-constructed buildings which are resistant to high winds. When a cyclone hits a poor fishing village, it is nearly always a disaster: tin roofs are stripped off bamboo dwellings like autumn leaves off a tree. The millions of people affected by disasters between 1991 and 1995 were predominantly the rural poor.

CDRC has identified several 'areas of vulnerability'. The first, and the most significant, concerns geographical events such as earthquakes, volcanic eruptions, and typhoons. In the second category are the hazards and disasters which result from human activities. Flash floods and landslides, for example, are frequently caused by deforestation. Forests act like a sponge, trapping the rain when it falls and releasing it slowly over the ensuing months. Once the land has been stripped bare, the water can rush unimpeded down the hillsides, causing landslides on steeper slopes and floods in the plains. Government figures suggest that one hectare of forest is being lost every minute in the Philippines, or some 10,000 hectares a week, much through illegal felling. According to CDRC, over a million people were affected by floods in 1994 and again in 1995.

CDRC's figures also include those who have been displaced by fighting between government forces, the New Peoples' Army, and the Muslim guerilla forces in Mindanao. The NPA is no longer the force it once was, and with the advent of an uneasy peace in Mindanao the number affected by military activity has declined, from around 170,000 in 1991 to 34,000 by 1995. However, CDRC and other organisations involved in disaster relief are concerned that a new form of displacement is on the increase. Dams, roads, mining projects, and other schemes which are loosely or explicitly associated with *Philippines 2000* are driving people from their homes. Again, figures are hard to come by, but the

Nonoy Regalado/ Oxfam

right Temporary shelter built by a family whose home was destroyed by *lahar*.

Ecumenical Commission for Displaced Families and Communities calculated that between January and October 1995 over 38,000 families were permanently displaced. This figure was 34 per cent higher than for the whole of 1994.

Coping with Pinatubo

The terminology used to classify the victims of Pinatubo's mudflows is chillingly impersonal. Those displaced by the initial flows in 1991 are known as *lahar* 1, those by the second year's as *lahar* 2, and so on. In June 1996 the villagers of Alasas were expecting, shortly, to become *lahar* 6. Sitting in the porch of a well-appointed house on the leafy main street, Paquito Timbol, former secretary to the *barangay* captain, reflects on the impending disaster: 'I've been here since 1946 and I've never worried about this community till now.' He motions in the distance of Mount Pinatubo, obscured now by heavy rain clouds, and says: 'If you go two kilometres up there you'll find what's left of Dolores Concepcion. That village was destroyed last year.'

The people of Alasas — 1,967 individuals in all — had been told to expect at least 10 feet of *lahar* once the monsoons arrived. A local organisation, the Pampanga Disaster Response Network, had helped the community to prepare its evacuation plans and everyone knew what they had to do once the alert was sounded. 'We've been assigned an evacuation centre,' explains a woman who has been working on what is cumbersomely termed disaster preparedness, 'and we expect to be there for the whole *lahar* season, longer if the damage is as bad as we expect.' She adds that most of the people in Alasas have lived here all their lives and know no other home. The *lahar* was going to swallow up their fields and houses and, like their erstwhile neighbours in Dolores Concepcion, they were about to experience the uncertain and often miserable existence of Pinatubo's refugees.

When Pinatubo erupted, having lain dormant for 500 years, experts estimated that disruption to life would continue for ten years. It now appears that this was an optimistic estimate; it is likely that *lahar* flows and floods will continue to cause chaos in the region for at least 15 years, until all the *lahar* has been washed off the mountains, either into the sea, where it has already smothered vast expanses of coral, or onto flat land, where it will stabilise. In purely economic terms the volcano has been a disaster for Central Luzon. Some 350,000 hectares of productive land have been covered with *lahar* and are virtually useless.

The cost in human terms can be most clearly seen in the evacuation centres. These are supposed to provide temporary accommodation for evacuees, who will eventually return to their villages or be housed in permanent resettlement sites managed by the government's Mount Pinatubo Commission (MPC).

Prior to Typhoon Mameng, MPC had resettled 34,550 families in permanent sites in Pampanga, but over 7,400 families were still waiting in evacuation centres. The backlog rose dramatically after the typhoon. At the beginning of 1996, 21,900 families — around 100,000 people — were living in temporary evacuation centres.

Waiting for help

Malino looks incongruously like an urban slum pitched into good fertile countryside: tin-roof bunkhouses simmer in the midday heat beneath a forest of TV aerials. Most of the 167 families in the centre saw their *barangay* partially disappear beneath the mudflows of 1994. Some returned to their homes in the dry season, but they were driven out again in 1995 when the *lahar* destroyed Bacolor town.

The bunkhouses were constructed by a Catholic organisation, SACOP, on land leased from the expatriate brother of Malino's *barangay* captain. The evacuation centre is administered by a 13-member evacuation centre management committee (ECME), all of whom are

women. Its co-ordinator, Cristina Turla, speaks with warmth and gratitude about the Pampanga Disaster Response Network (PDRN), which rescued them when the *lahar* came and helped establish the management committee. There was little that PDRN could do, however, to improve the physical conditions within the centre. 'There's a big problem with overcrowding,' explains Cristina as she shows us a room 15 feet square. 'This is the space every family has to live in. Some have seven children, so you can imagine what it's like.' The bunkhouses are ill-ventilated and oppressively hot and there is little space between them.

In such conditions infectious diseases associated with poor hygiene are a serious problem. Overcrowding can also lead to tension. 'Maybe one family makes too much noise,' says Cristina, 'but we can normally settle disputes by talking to people.' Considering the living conditions, she adds, there were relatively few social problems in the centre. Indeed, hardship had encouraged people to help one another. 'If there's a family with a serious problem,' explains Cristina, 'such as no money to buy food, or someone's very sick, we'll go round the centre and get contributions from other people.'

The women on the management committee had no idea how long they would remain in Malino. 'What if the owner comes back from Canada and says he wants the land?' asks one rhetorically. Another speculates that they might be here for ten years or more: 'But we haven't lost hope,' she adds swiftly. 'Someone, some day, might resettle us.'

Does she mean the government?

This question elicits bitter laughter. 'We understand that there are other communities whose needs are greater than ours,' says Cristina, choosing her words carefully, 'but the government and the Mount Pinatubo Commission have been very slow, very inefficient. There are still evacuees from 1991 who haven't been resettled yet.'

right Local people inspecting the Fidel Ramos mega-dyke. Many feel the money to build it could have been better used for resettlement schemes.

Apathy and incompetence

The Mount Pinatubo Commission claims that its resettlement programme is well managed and that the number of evacuees waiting for places in permanent sites is relatively small. This is simply not the case. Over 20,000 families in Pampanga alone were languishing in school halls and temporary evacuation centres as the 1996 monsoon approached; another typhoon, another disastrous *lahar* season, and their numbers would swell dramatically.

Yet again, land reform — or the lack of it — is the main issue. It is not penury, but political apathy, which is responsible for the lack of resettlement sites. No one in a position of influence or power has been prepared to tackle the land issue. In Pampanga there are ten landlords who own between 1000 and 5000 hectares each. None has relinquished, or been made to relinquish, the smallest portion of land to help resettle the victims of Pinatubo.

From time to time the MPC has established resettlement sites which evacuees have spurned, generally on the grounds that they are too remote. One such site is to be found half way up Mount Arayat, some 29 kilometres from San Fernando, the nearest place where people can expect to find work. Public transport to and from Mount Arayat costs 70 pesos a day; a day-labourer is paid around 130 pesos a day. There are no schools near the resettlement site and the facilities are poor. Little wonder, then, that many of those offered places there have refused to go.

Rather than tackle the land issue, the government has made some grand and costly gestures, one of which is the Fidel B. Ramos mega-dyke, a 17-kilometre wall whose purpose is to channel *lahar* away from Angeles City and San Fernando. The project was controversial from the outset. It has pleased the business interests in San Fernando, but outraged many of the village communities which have lost land to the dyke, or who now believe that they are in greater danger of being submerged because of it. Whether the dyke will work remains to be seen. Independent engineers claim that it has been so badly designed that *lahar* flows similar to those of 1995 would certainly breach it. The dyke was a political solution to a technical problem, and a very expensive one too, costing 2.75 billion pesos, or around $100 million. It is money, say the victims of Pinatubo, that could have been much better spent.

Life in a resettlement site

Not long ago the countryside between Tokwing and Angeles City was a verdant patchwork of cane fields and rice paddy, interspersed with small villages with tree-lined streets and clusters of palm and mango. Now it is a lunar landscape, a wasteland of grey *lahar*. Here and there scraps of tin roof or thatch poke through the mud, and a line of telegraph poles — now waist-high — marks the course of a road which lies buried under 15 feet of volcanic debris. One of the villages submerged by the *lahar* was Mancatian, whose houses were washed away in 1994. Many of its former inhabitants are now to be found in Tokwing resettlement site, and here, as in Malino, it is the women who have done most to improve conditions and get the best they can from the government agencies. Their menfolk are too busy trying to earn a living in Angeles City, and some are far away, in Manila and beyond.

'We feel we're constantly having to battle against the authorities,' explains Yolly de la Cruz, who is the chair of the local chapter of Ugnayan, an alliance of Pinatubo's victims. When Yolly arrived she and many other families were lodged in huts beside a large productivity centre. The huts, which are now home to 194 families, are cramped, dirty, ill-served in every sense, and surrounded by pools of stagnant water. The productivity centre, in contrast, consists of rows of gleaming white warehouses. These were constructed to attract industry to the resettlement sites, and therefore provide jobs for the people here. The warehouses in Tokwing remain empty; productivity centres throughout the region have proved to be expensive white elephants. The industries which were supposed to move in require skilled labour, whereas most of those in the resettlement centres are farmers, skilled in handicraft production perhaps, but not in computer technology.

By mid-1996 the resettlement site was taking on the attributes of permanency: some families had attached their homes, illegally, to the electricity supply; some had constructed hen coops, added porticos, and planted flowers and shrubs. 'If it hadn't been for us, there'd have been no progress,' explains Yolly. 'We only got water pumps installed because we campaigned for them.' She adds that many people were angry about the way in which the units have been allocated. Often the least deserving — including friends and relatives of local officials — had been given units ahead of the more needy.

Visit any of the evacuation and resettlement sites around Pinatubo and you will hear a similar story. It is the evacuees themselves who are doing most to improve conditions, often with little or no help from the authorities. And it is the women who are at the forefront of the organisations which are fighting for better conditions and helping the least fortunate and the poorest to survive.

below Heavy rain floods this evacuation site at Tokwing, which was built cheaply and quickly, without proper drainage or sanitation.

Nonoy Regalado/ Oxfam

Nonoy Regalado / Oxfam

Building for the future

Soon after it was set up in 1984, the Citizens' Disaster Response Centre, whose headquarters is in Manila, decided to establish a regional network to respond to specific disasters. There are now 18 regional centres making up the Citizens' Disaster Response Network (CDRN) and their function is to promote citizenry-based development-oriented disaster response, or CBDODR. The centre in Luzon is known as CONCERN, the Central Luzon Disaster Response Network, and it comprises a number of separate offices, one being PDRN, the Pampanga Disaster Response Network, which became operational in the months before Pinatubo erupted.

PDRN and its counterparts in other provinces have helped to organise evacuation procedures, dispensed emergency food aid, given psycho-social debriefing to displaced families, provided training in disaster preparedness, and lobbied the government on issues ranging from housing to health care. They have played a significant role in the relief process, but they have failed to influence the decision-makers in matters of lasting strategic importance, the most obvious being the need for land reform and for a viable and better organised resettlement programme.

Following the 1995 typhoon, CDRC agreed to oversee the construction of bunkhouses which would eventually provide temporary homes for 1000 families displaced from San Juan. It took six months to find a site, some distance away in Mexico village.

'We said right from the beginning this is not just a CDRC project,' explains its social services officer, Malu Fellizar-Cagay. 'It's a joint venture between CDRC and the community of San Juan.' A points system established which families were most in need of resettlement. The widows, the elderly, the disabled, those who had lost everything in the *lahar,* and those who had no breadwinners, were deemed to be in greatest need and were allocated bunkhouse accommodation. This was in stark contrast to the way in which the government generally allocates accommodation in evacuation resettlement sites: those with good political contacts, or cash to spare, generally go to the top of the queue.

The bunkhouses have been designed to a standard which far surpasses those constructed under government schemes. Each will house six families, and each family will have 21 square metres of floor space, with a door at either end and two windows. The World Health Organisation's emergency guidelines stipulate that there should be one latrine for 20 people. In the Mexico evacuation centre each bunkhouse is to be served by two latrines and two bathrooms and there will be a nine-metre space between the rows of bunkhouses.

This was the first project in the Philippines to involve disaster victims in the building of their own homes, and all those who were capable of useful work were being encouraged to participate. 'We've tried to ensure that there's one skilled carpenter to each bunkhouse,' explains Malu, on a site inspection in mid-July. Over 100 people were working in teams on the bunkhouses, some of which were nearing completion.

The bunkhouses are not a final solution. They will provide temporary accommodation for *lahar* victims, and as some leave — either to return to their land or to other resettlement sites — others will take their place. There is no land available nearby and therefore no opportunity for people to make a living as farmers, which many once were. The projects will only help a small proportion of Pinatubo's victims. All the same, it has put the rhetoric of self-help — or citizenry-based development-oriented disaster response — into action, and it may well become a model for the future. The government and the MPC will find it far harder to argue that their evacuation centres are adequate when they compare so unfavourably to the Mexico bunkhouses.

left People displaced by the Pinatubo disaster mixing cement for the construction of new bunkhouses, Mexico village.

Strategies for survival

Nonoy Regalado/ Oxfam

Sally Jeffrey/ Oxfam

above (top) At school in Tugas village, northern Mindanao. Literacy rates are high in the Philippines, though children from rural areas spend fewer years in school, on average, than their urban compatriots.

above (bottom) Drop-in centre for prostitutes in Davao.

Poverty is an overwhelmingly rural phenomenon in the Philippines although to a visitor the endless slums in urban Manila, when contrasted with the picturesque nature of much of the countryside, might suggest the exact opposite. Life expectancy in the NCR, the National Capital Region, which includes Metro Manila, is 68.6 years; in remote Central Mindanao, it is 13 years less. There is 99.1 per cent literacy in the NCR; 83 per cent literacy in Central Mindanao. Children in the NCR spend an average 9.7 years at school; in Central Mindanao they spend 5.8 years. The poverty index developed by the Philippine Human Development Network is low for the NCR, at 14.9, and exceptionally high, over 50, for Central Mindanao. The poorest regions tend to be the most remote and politically troubled; the more affluent are generally close to the capital.

Poverty is as much about lack of options as it is about lack of cash. Many of the rural poor simply stay where they are, eking out a living as best they can in the hope their situation will eventually improve. But others — and in the Philippines a significant number — adopt survival strategies which involve physical movement. Some are ambitious; some are desperate. Either way, they see migration as a means to improving their standard of living.

For many, the escape from poverty means both a change of occupation and a change of address. This is most clearly seen in the red-light districts of places like Manila, Angeles City, Olongapo, and Cebu. UNICEF estimates that there are half a million prostitutes in the Philippines, a fifth of whom are minors, some as young as six years old. A survey carried out by UNICEF found that 50 per cent of the prostitutes interviewed had entered the sex trade to escape poverty, which more often than not meant rural poverty; a further 15 per cent were fleeing family problems — broken marriages, loss of a parent and so on; eight per cent had been physically forced into prostitution, and only three per cent claimed that they had chosen prostitution as an easy way to earn money. The Philippines has now become a major destination for paedophiles and foreigners are increasingly active in running the sex industry. Over half the bars along Angeles City's notorious Field Avenue are now owned and managed by Australians.

Poverty has also turned rural Philippines into a huge exporter of cheap labour. There are an estimated 6.2 million overseas contract workers (OCWs), many of whom have village backgrounds. Human rights organisations have become increasingly worried about the maltreatment meted out to many Filipinos, particularly those working as domestic servants in Singapore, Japan, and the Middle East. However, the government is reluctant to take any steps which might lead to a loss of the considerable revenue OCWs bring into the country. Between them they remit around $4.7 billion a year, equivalent in 1996 to around 20 per cent of export earnings. This inflow of money is economically significant for two reasons. First, it stimulates consumer spending; one in three Filipino families is now said to be partially dependent on OCWs remittances. Second, the government receives substantial taxes from OCW remittances, equivalent to around $34 million a year.

In 1960 less than a third of the population lived in urban areas. Now almost half does. Landlessness and low

below Looking for materials for recycling, on a Patayas garbage dump in Quezon City.

wages have driven millions of families out of the countryside and into the cities. This book began with the story of Hernari Monares. In his view it made better economic sense to live the life of an urban scavenger than to work as a day-labourer on farms in the countryside. His story is typical of millions. The housemaid working in Singapore or the Gulf, the prostitute working in the girlie bars of Olongapo, and the men and women who live and scavenge on the garbage dumps in Metro Manila have one thing in common: they have been driven from their homes by poverty, poverty which has its roots in the inequitable distribution of land and resources.

President Ramos bluntly stated in a speech on land reform: 'Poverty in our country is, in the end, rural poverty.' The key to its eradication, in his view and others, is land reform. Sadly, his deeds have not matched his words and for most Filipino peasants land reform remains a distant dream. This is not to say that individuals and communities cannot improve their lot without land reform. The basket-makers of Pangasinan are among the many small communities who are proving that ingenuity, hard work, and good organisation can help to raise living standards for people in the countryside.

Bridging the poverty gap

Sison village looks like a rural idyll. Bamboo huts are scattered beneath a canopy of palm and fruit trees beside a winding stream. Pigs and hens wander unrestrained around the sandy alleys and opposite Renato Velasco's home scores of pigeons gently coo from a homemade cote. A powerful, big-boned man with a beguilingly soft voice, Renato came to Pangasinan province from Pampanga in 1968. Initially he made a living as a street vendor in the towns, then in 1976 he married into a family involved in the craft business. 'I carried on trading,' he explains, 'but my wife and her family

taught me to make the baskets, so I did more and more of that.' In 1978 they had the first of their six children; as the years past and the family grew they found it increasingly difficult to make ends meet. However, their fortunes have recently changed.

'Before 1993 most of the basket-makers in the village were lucky if they made 3000 pesos a month,' recalls Renato. 'Now, we make 4000 or so. I've started making improvements to our house and my children can now go onto higher-level education. I wouldn't be able to clothe my children as I do on my old wages.'

A few kilometres away is the village of Bonapal. Under a lean-to roof a dozen women and teenage girls sit in the shade, their fingers expertly weaving bamboo reeds into rattan frames. Unlike the basket-makers of Sison, they have only recently learnt the skills of the craft. They began making baskets in 1990, explains the treasurer of their social production unit, Betty Estayo, but they made little money during the first three years.

The turning point, both for the basket-makers of Bonapal and Sison, came in 1993. Before then the trade was dominated by a small number of suppliers. The suppliers, most of whom were also frame-makers, received orders from abroad through the Community Crafts Association of the Philippines (CCAP). A system of patronage meant that the suppliers favoured some producers but not others. The women of Bonapal did badly under the old dispensation, as did many of the men and women in Sison; they were not well-connected. The suppliers, of whom there were 17 in all, also took a slice of the producers' profits. For example, CCAP would pay 73 pesos for the magazine organisers which were sold in Oxfam shops in Britain. The suppliers would pass 57 pesos to the producers, and keep 16 pesos themselves. Some made up to 17,000 pesos a year, five times more than the most prosperous producers.

Those days have gone. CCAP disbanded the old structures in 1993 and insisted that it would only do business with democratically run social production units (SPUs), of which there are now seven in Pangasinan province.

'In the early years,' explains Betty Estayo, 'we were lucky if we made 200 pesos a month. Now we make at least 1,000 each.' In the early years the women all had to work as casual labour on farms. 'Farm work is hell,' says Cecilia Vergara, the SPU president, 'and now that this brings us a living, we don't need to work in the fields any more.'

Prior to 1993 the basket-making business was seen as precisely that — a business. Some — the suppliers — did very well out of it; others — the producers — did not. Since the social production units were established, all members have had an equal say in the management of the trade. Orders are now equitably distributed among the members of each SPU. No fortunes are being made, but community-level democracy has ensured that all get a fair return for their work.

Now the profits made from the basket trade are being used for the common good. In 1993 Zenaida Quismorio, the new executive director of CCAP, set up a department to promote development projects among the craft workers. The SPUs were encouraged to put aside a slice of their profits and use the common funds for social projects. By February 1996 Riverside SPU at Sison had a common fund worth 10,000 pesos. Members can now take out low-interest loan; some use these to buy livestock, others buy essential household items. At Bonapal the women have built up a common fund which is used to buy materials for basket-making and as a source of individual loans. It has proved especially useful for those women who have needed money to pay for the treatment of sick children. At another village nearby, Dilan, the SPU has used its common fund to buy a calf and a young buffalo. The former will provide

above Basket-makers at Dilan village.

milk when it matures; the latter will be used to plough the small plots of land which the members own.

The male members of Dilan and Riverside SPUs claim that the women are treated as equals and have as much say in the running of the units as the men. This is the theory. The practice is somewhat different: nearly always the women defer to the men, and it is the latter who make the important decisions. It was for this reason that the women of Bonapal decided to set themselves up as a women's group. 'Actually,' says Betty Estayo, 'one of the husbands, a framer, was a member for a while. He taught us a lot, but he's left now — he found us too gossipy!' The women are adamant that they are better off without the men. 'We feel far less inhibited when there are no men around,' says one. 'We can discuss things far more openly among ourselves. If a husband and a wife are together, the man speaks up, the woman doesn't. That's the culture here.' Betty Estayo adds that the work of the social production unit has helped to raise the women's self-esteem — 'It shows that we can run things as well as the men' — and it has raised their status in the eyes of their husbands. 'It also means that we can contribute towards looking after our families,' she adds. 'That means a lot for us.'

The craft workers of Pangasinan stress that although they are better off than they used to be, their financial situation is far from secure. For one thing, they operate in a market where tastes change. A magazine organiser or rattan basket that sells well in England one year may go out of fashion the next. The producers have to accept this and come up with new designs to attract the foreign buyers. At Sison they have done precisely that. When they were told that their magazine racks were no longer selling, they designed a new one, which is proving successful.

More worrying, in many ways, than the uncertainties of the market are the spiralling costs of raw materials. In Dilan, the vice-president of the SPU, Danilo Salcedo, rapidly enumerates the present cost of materials for a hamper: four rattan poles at 7.20 pesos; three bundles of bamboo at 16.50 pesos; wooden spokes at 19.50 pesos; seven metres of rope for four pesos; glue, nails and electricity at ten pesos. Total 95 pesos. 'And the price we get for a hamper is 130 pesos,' concludes Danilo. 'The weavers get ten pesos and the framers 25 pesos. Last year we also got 130 pesos a hamper, but the raw materials were cheaper then, so the weavers and framers got more.' He estimates that over the last 12 months raw materials have risen in cost by 30 per cent, while the price which CCAP are paying for goods has scarcely risen in seven years.

In Bonapal the women are especially concerned about the rising cost of education. 'My husband's away at sea,' explains Betty Estayo, 'so we're better off than most and we can afford to educate our children.' They have three in college and one at high school. 'But for many of the women here it's far more difficult. It used to cost 65 pesos a year to send a child to school; now it costs 300 pesos.'

In addition to the annual fees, parents must pay for books, uniforms, and transport, all of which have become more expensive. A family with three children at school pays around 600 pesos a month, rather more than half what the women can earn from basket-making. However, the women concede that they would be much worse off if it were not for the social production units and the money they make from the craft trade.

A tale of two cities

right Rich and poor Filipinos live side by side, but inhabit different worlds.

In rural areas in the Philippines the average annual population growth between 1965 and 1995 was 1.8 per cent; in the cities it was 3.9 per cent. These figures are not so much a reflection of varying fecundity as of the rural exodus, which has had a dramatic impact on Manila in particular. During the 1980s, its population grew at the rate of four per cent a year and its living conditions compare unfavourably with those of most major metropolises. In Manila an average three people share each room, the same as in Calcutta, double the number for Cairo and six times more than in New York or Los Angeles.

Smoky Mountain, the garbage dump in Manila which was once home to Hernari Monares and his family, provides a parable for modern times. Until 1995, 4,000 families made a living on the dump and its infamy was such that it even attracted guided tours for Japanese tourists. It was a blight on the urban landscape and a living reproach to successive governments, who endured its presence but made no move to help its inhabitants. *Philippines 2000*, however, has come up with an answer. A private company has been granted title to the land on condition that it reclaims 40 hectares of Manila bay which lie beside it. The land will be used for warehouse storage by Japanese and Taiwanese companies, and Smoky Mountain will be turned into a commercial reprocessing site. As part of the deal with the municipal authorities, the company has agreed to use some of its profits to rehouse displaced families. A new housing development will be jointly managed with the National Housing Authority, which claims that this is a model for the future.

The inhabitants of Smoky Mountain were largely unimpressed by the housing offer, rightly so it now seems. Those families who accepted the offer are living in tented camps some four hours' drive to the south, near Cavite, far from potential places of employment. Those families who declined to leave Smoky Mountain, and they were the majority, were violently evicted. The leader of their resistance movement was murdered by soldiers.

Between the dump and reclamation site the main road passes over a river. Hanging from the bridge, like wooden nest boxes, are the homes of 16 families — some 75 people. The squatters of Marcello-under-the-Bridge have no electricity, no piped water, and no sanitation other than the river below their shacks, which they use as a sewer, which it closely resembles. There are flies everywhere and the hanging shacks are dark and cramped. One of the women, Rowena Banez, says that despite the dreadful living conditions, the families here have a certain attachment to the place. 'We're better off than some others I can think of,' she says, 'but our major problem is insecurity.' The government is threatening to evict the squatters who live along the road which serves as Marcello-under-the-Bridge's roof, and Rowena and her community anticipate that they will be the next to go after that. 'We simply

below Squatter home at Marcello-under-the Bridge

don't know where we could move to,' she says with a resigned shrug.

The squatters at Marcello-under-the-Bridge are admirably industrious. Some of them work in the construction business as labourers, others work as street vendors, and now and again the men hire a *banca* and go fishing in Manila Bay. The families all value education highly, although they can scarcely afford the fees and books and uniforms. 'We realise,' explains Rolly Banez, who runs a small stall beside the bridge, 'that it if our children are going to have a chance of getting decent jobs, they'll need to finish their schooling.' He adds that the nearest school is many miles away and transport costs 10 pesos a day for each child. 'If a family hasn't got any money,' says Rowena, 'then the mother will get up at 4am and walk the children all the way to the school.'

In the National Capital Region over 3.5 million have a story to tell similar to Rowena's: they live in slums, struggle to survive, and in many cases are worried about insecurity, not least because they are excluded from the brave new world of *Philippines 2000* and may eventually be evicted to make way for its projects. Especially vulnerable are the quarter of a million families who live along railway tracks, *esteros* and in areas earmarked for infrastructure projects.

Manila is a city in crisis, or rather it is two cities, one for the rich, one for the poor. The lifestyles and consumer aspirations of the middle class would not seem out of place in Dallas, while there is poverty here to match anything which can be seen in Africa. Metro Manila suffers from chronic overcrowding, poor services, worsening pollution, and a spiralling crime rate, all of which, to a greater or lesser degree, are a reflection of the flight from rural poverty and of the gross inequities which exist between rich and poor, between landowner and peasant, between the well-connected and the powerless.

Nonoy Regalado / Oxfam

In search of justice

Noroy Regalado/ Oxfam

left young street seller, Manila

The Philippines has a vibrant and sophisticated network of non-governmental organisations (NGOs). While some campaign for policy change, others work with poor and marginalised communities. A few do both. Many NGOs grew out of the movements which opposed the dictatorial rule of President Marcos. Many, inevitably, became highly politicised and formed close links with the then-banned Communist Party. Some NGOs and peoples' organisations have retained their links and have been affected by the recent split within the Party. Some have aligned themselves with the 'reaffirmists', whose analysis of what is wrong in Philippine society remains fundamentally unchanged, as does their belief in the importance of an armed struggle. Others have chosen to support factions whose approaches range from selective use of violent means to peaceful lobbying and the establishment of a strong and uncorrupt civic society. 'The great debate', as it is portentously referred to, has been highly divisive and it has affected the work of many organisations and coalitions. However, it would be wrong to overstate its importance; most of those who work in the voluntary sector have nothing to do with the political machinations of the Communist Party.

NGOs have been especially effective where they have focused on the sustainable use of resources, and there is no doubt that their work among fishing and tribal people in particular is helping to conserve resources — fish, timber, agricultural land — for future generations. Where the NGOs have been less successful is in challenging a political system which is responsible for enhancing divisions between rich and poor, rather than doing away with them, although they were a significant force during the EDSA revolution.

Politics in the Philippines is about gold, goons, and guns — wealth and power. In theory, the Philippines is the only true democracy in South-East Asia, but it scarcely deserves the name. Out of the 228 elected senators and congressmen, all but a dozen are dollar-millionaires. Many are multi-millionaires, and their wealth, in many cases, is based on the ownership of land. Little wonder, then, that so little has been done in the field of land reform. Little wonder that there is such strong opposition to the Fisheries Code, when so many congressmen own trawlers and prawn farms.

In theory, poor Filipinos could vote for virtuous, altruistic men and women who would champion their cause and create a more just society. But *trapo* politics is deeply engrained in the Filipino psyche, and the relationship between politician and voter is a mirror of that between landlord and peasant. The peasant always hopes that the landlord will come to his aid in times of trouble. Generally speaking, he will. He will pay for the sick wife to go to hospital; he will send round a few bags of rice when crops fail. This helps to maintain the master-servant relationship, which suits the master better than it does the servant. In a wider context feudal patronage becomes political patronage. A combination of philanthropy, charisma, and terror is enough to keep most politicians in power, and as long as this system persists it is difficult to see how a fairer society can be created.

It is too early to judge whether *Philippines 2000* will succeed in turning the country into an economic tiger, and whether it will spark off long-term sustainable growth. It is clear, however, that *Philippines 2000* and its codicil, the Social Reform Agenda, have done little to challenge the inherent inequities in Philippine society. Land reform must still come top of any reformist agenda, but tax reform is equally important. The present tax system penalises the poor: while they are forced to pay value-added taxes on food, cooking oil, clothes and other essential goods, the rich have proved themselves to be geniuses when it comes to avoiding personal taxes. Tax evasion is costing the country over $3 billion a year, equivalent to two-thirds of the money remitted each year by the country's 6 million overseas contract workers.

The champions of justice have much to rail against still, but in certain respects life has changed for the better in the Philippines. Ten years ago, under President Marcos, all opposition to the government was ruthlessly suppressed. Under Cory Aquino, there were marginal improvements, in terms of human rights if not the economy, but nothing was done to change the feudal system of land tenure. Unlike his predecessors, President Ramos has realised that the NGO movement, and peoples' organisations which operate in the community, should have some say in the formulation of government policy. NGOs are now regularly consulted over the drafting of the Fisheries Code, and the Legal Rights and Natural Resources Centre (LRC) has been intimately involved in drafting the Ancestral Domain Bill, which should be of benefit to indigenous people when it becomes law.

Furthermore, individuals who were once a thorn in the government's side are now to be found in positions of influence within the civil service. Antonio La Vina, for example, was formerly the executive director of LRC; now he is an under-secretary in the Department of Environment and Natural Resources (DENR). He concedes that there are many problems facing the department: 'It's difficult to bring about rapid change in a bureaucracy that's been here for 100 years,' he says, 'but we are changing things for the better.' He believes that the rhetoric of community-based resource management, much loved by politicians nowadays, is more than rhetoric: for example, there have been tangible improvements in forestry practices. Since he joined the legal affairs department, corrupt officials have been disciplined and dismissed and the department has become much more vigorous in imposing pollution laws.

If DENR is reforming itself, then some of the credit must go to the organisations who have brought pressure to bear on government. 'There's no doubt in my mind,' says La Vina, 'that the NGO movement is very significant in terms of getting change.' The NGO movement has done much to improve resource management at the local level; now it must become part of the struggle to create a strong civic society — a society which will do away with the unjust structures which are primarily responsible for the poverty which affects over half of the population.

below basketball is played all over the Philippines, even in remote villages

The Philippines: facts and figures

Nonoy Regalado / Oxfam

above Tugas village, Danao bay is typical of the small settlements that line the coast of the Philippines

Area: 29,817,000 ha

Population: 69.26 million (1995)

Percentage of population living in urban areas: 45.7

Population growth rate: 2.07%

Gross Domestic Product (GDP): 1905.3 billion pesos

GDP growth (1995): 4.9%

GDP per capita: $1,083

Total external debt: $42.2 billion (1995)

Debt servicing as percentage of export revenues: 13%

Net inward investment from abroad: $2.4 billion (1995)

Remittances from Philippine nationals working abroad: $4 billion per year

Uncollected taxes: Approximately $3 billion per year

Adult literacy: 90%

Life expectancy at birth: 65

Infant mortality 1990-5 projection: 40 per 1,000 live births

Under 5 mortality: 62 per 1,000

Religion: 85% Catholic; 4% Protestant; remainder Muslim or Animist.

Currency conversion: $1 = P26.18 (September 1996)

Sources
'Philippines Survey', *Financial Times*, 18 September 1996
World Resources 1994-95, World Resources Institute, 1994, OUP
Far Eastern Economics Review.

Oxfam in the Philippines

Nonoy Regalado / Oxfam

Oxfam (United Kingdom and Ireland) has been funding projects in the Philippines for more than 20 years but an office was set up only ten years ago, shortly after the downfall of the Marcos regime.

In a country with tens of thousands of NGOs and other grassroots initiatives, there has never been a lack of potential partners. It is partly because of this diverse and sizeable NGO community that Oxfam, at an early stage, saw the need to focus on a limited number of causes, targeting groups which still had difficulty articulating their needs, and for whom external funding was largely absent. An early decision was made to focus on groups working with coastal or indigenous communities, or with groups set up by those communities. Women and their gender needs were also identified as a main focus of Oxfam's funding and non-funding support. A major earthquake in the north of the country in 1990, the eruption of Mount Pinatubo in 1991, made Oxfam decide to work with communities on disaster preparedness and disaster management. The Oxfam programme also involves advice and marketing support for small-scale crafts producers.

Oxfam is now one out of many agencies, both local and international, with a primary concern for fishing communities and indigenous people. Oxfam's long association with these groups has led to a better understanding of such issues as land rights, gender relations and sustainable resource management, hence the important role of non-funding support. Building local capacity on disaster preparedness remains an important component of Oxfam's

work. In fact, building local capacity is the unifying theme in all of Oxfam's Philippines programme. This ranges from training in leadership skills for women, to the development of effective advocacy strategies to ensure that basic rights of local people are met and that they can have a say in their future.

Further reading

Bautista, G M (1994) *Natural Resources, Economic Development and the State: The Philippines Experience*, Institute of South-East Asian Studies.

Bauzon, K E (1991) *Liberalism and the Quest for Islamic Identity in the Philippines*, Acorn Press.

Brands, H W (1992) *Bound to Empire: The US and the Philippines*, Oxford University Press.

Broad, R and Cavanagh, J (1993) *Plundering Paradise: The Struggle for the Environment in the Philippines*, University of California Press.

Human Rights Watch (1996) *Human Rights and Forest Management in the 1990s*.

Hutchcroft, P D (1996) *The Philippines at the Crossroads: Sustaining Political and Economic Reform*, Asia Society.

Kunio, Y (1994) *The Nation and Economic Growth: The Philippines and Thailand*, Oxford University Press.

McMullen, V (1992) *Looking at the Philippines Through the Eyes of the Poor*, CAFOD.

Pertierra, R (1994) *Cultures and Texts: Representations of Philippine Society*, University of the Philippines Press.

Phelan, J L (1959) *The Hispanisation of the Philippines: Spanish Aims and Filipino Responses, 1565-1700*, University of Wisconsin Press.

Rivera, T C (1996) *Philippines: State of the Nation*, Institute of South-East Asian Studies.

Roces A R and Roces G (1992) *Culture Shock!: Philippines*, Kuperard.

Steinberg, D J (1994) *The Philippines: A Singular and a Plural Place*, Westview Press.

Thompson, W S (1992) *The Philippines in Crisis: Development and Security in the Aquino Era*, St Martins Press.

Oxfam (UK and Ireland) publishes a wide range of books, manuals, and resource materials for specialist, academic, and general readers. For a free catalogue, please write to:

Oxfam Publishing
274 Banbury Road
Oxford OX2 7DZ, UK.

telephone: (0)1865 313922.
e-mail: publish@oxfam.org.uk

Oxfam publications are available from the following agents:

for Canada and the USA:
Humanities Press International, 165 First Avenue, Atlantic Highlands, New Jersey NJ 07716-1289, USA;
tel. (908)872 1441; fax (908) 872 0717

for Southern Africa:
David Philip Publishers, PO Box 23408, Claremont, Cape Town 7735, South Africa;
tel. (021) 64 4136; fax (021) 64 3358.